Pro Multithrea[ ]
Memory Management
for iOS and OS X

■ ■ ■

Kazuki Sakamoto
Tomohiko Furumoto

Apress®

Pro Multithreading and Memory Management for iOS and OS X

ISBN-13 (pbk): 978-1-4302-4116-4

ISBN-13 (electronic): 978-1-4302-4117-1

Trademarked names, logos, and images may appear in this book. Rather than use a trademark symbol with every occurrence of a trademarked name, logo, or image we use the names, logos, and images only in an editorial fashion and to the benefit of the trademark owner, with no intention of infringement of the trademark.

The use in this publication of trade names, trademarks, service marks, and similar terms, even if they are not identified as such, is not to be taken as an expression of opinion as to whether or not they are subject to proprietary rights.

While the advice and information in this book are believed to be true and accurate at the date of publication, neither the authors nor the editors nor the publisher can accept any legal responsibility for any errors or omissions that may be made. The publisher makes no warranty, express or implied, with respect to the material contained herein.

President and Publisher: Paul Manning
Lead Editor: Michelle Lowman
Development Editor: Jim Markham
Technical Reviewer: Paul Chapman, Mark Makdad, Ross Sharrott
Translator: Tomohiko Furumoto
Editorial Board: Steve Anglin, Ewan Buckingham, Gary Cornell, Louise Corrigan, Morgan Ertel, Jonathan Gennick, Jonathan Hassell, Robert Hutchinson, Michelle Lowman, James Markham, Matthew Moodie, Jeff Olson, Jeffrey Pepper, Douglas Pundick, Ben Renow-Clarke, Dominic Shakeshaft, Gwenan Spearing, Matt Wade, Tom Welsh
Coordinating Editor: Brent Dubi
Copy Editor: Valerie Greco
Compositor: MacPS,LLC
Indexer: SPi Global
Artist: Satoshi Ida
Cover Designer: Anna Ishchenko

Distributed to the book trade worldwide by Springer Science+Business Media New York, 233 Spring Street, 6th Floor, New York, NY 10013. Phone 1-800-SPRINGER, fax (201) 348-4505, e-mail orders-ny@springer-sbm.com, or visit www.springeronline.com.

For information on translations, please e-mail rights@apress.com, or visit www.apress.com.

Apress and friends of ED books may be purchased in bulk for academic, corporate, or promotional use. eBook versions and licenses are also available for most titles. For more information, reference our Special Bulk Sales–eBook Licensing web page at www.apress.com/bulk-sales.

Any source code or other supplementary materials referenced by the author in this text is available to readers at www.apress.com. For detailed information about how to locate your book's source code, go to www.apress.com/source-code.

Contents at a Glance

Contents

About the Author

Kazuki Sakamoto is a software engineer proud of his Stack Overflow reputation of more than 5,800. He has deep and diverse experience: seven years as a game programmer; five years as a UNIX kernel, device driver, and embedded software developer; five years as a mobile software engineer; five years as a mobile software engineer; and one year as a Web engineer. Additionally, Kazuki has ported NetBSD on BeBox, maintenance MacVim-KaoriYa, developed iPhone applications, and has written books such as the one you have in your hands. You can follow him on Twitter @splhack.

About the Translator

 **Tomohiko Furumoto** is a software engineer experienced as a game developer and mobile phone application engineer. You can follow him on Twitter @munakoiso.

About the Technical Reviewers

left to right: Mark Makdad, Paul Chapman, Ross Sharrott

Paul Chapman, **Mark Makdad**, and **Ross Sharrott** are three location independent, mobile developers who make up Long Weekend (www.longweekendmobile.com).

Paul is a 15-year software veteran. He previously founded cvMail, a SaaS startup acquired by Thomson Reuters in 2007, and was IT senior manager for a Japanese company in Tokyo. Paul is currently Adjunct Industry Fellow in Mobile Software at Australia's Swinburne University of Technology and sits on the University's ICT faculty advisory board.

Mark is a prolific web and mobile programmer, an experienced salesman, and Japanese/English bilingual. A graduate of the University of Illinois, he has co-authored multiple university-level courses on mobile programming and is very active in the smartphone technology scene in Tokyo.

Ross is an information systems professional with a strong interest in the world of finance. He has designed, implemented, and managed multimillion dollar IT systems and lead mission critical development efforts. A full-time developer of iOS and Android apps, he is based in New York and Tokyo.

Acknowledgments

I owe much to those who have contributed to this book. Takahashi-san of Tatsu-zine Publishing and Hatanaka-san of Impress Japan Corporation who kindly accepted my unexpected proposal for this book, for which I'll always be thankful. Thanks to Hata-san who gave me an inspirational start writing this book. Thanks to Ida-san, who took his time to work on all the great illustrations in this book. Samuli-san and Nozaki-san have kindly reviewed this book, which helped me a lot. Finally, thanks to Furumoto-san, who helped me extensively with the translation.

> *"I've always wanted to own and control the primary technology in everything we do."*
>
> — Steve Jobs

Without Steve's passion and technologies, this book couldn't exist. Thank you and rest in peace.

Introduction

Preface

This book is about ARC, Blocks, and Grand Central Dispatch in iOS and OS X. It's a bit different from other books. In short, this book is quite deep, and explains the following.

- ARC, a memory management mechanism newly introduced for iOS 5 and OS X Lion.

- Blocks and Grand Central Dispatch, introduced for iOS 4 and OS X Snow Leopard, are mainly for writing multithreaded applications.

These new technologies are essential to develop on iOS 5 and OS X Lion. Although they seem easy to understand, in fact, you will encounter pitfalls if you don't really master them. In this book, I explain them along with the Apple's source codes themselves so that you can have a deeper understanding than by just reading Apple's references.

Who This Book Is For

- Those who understand C/C++, but not much Objective-C

- Those who want to know how Objective-C source code works

- Those who develop iOS or Mac applications and want to know more so they can move up to a higher level

Chapter 1

Life Before Automatic Reference Counting

OSX Lion and iOS5 now offer an application memory management mechanism called Automatic Reference Counting (ARC). In short, ARC makes memory management the job of the compiler rather than the programmer, which quite often increases performance significantly.

In Chapters 2 and 3, you see just how powerful ARC is. But before entering such a dream world, it's best to review the basics of memory management in a non-ARC environment. In doing so, you'll form a greater appreciation of all that ARC has to offer and build a stronger foundation for when we delve into ARC in the next two chapters.

We start with an overview of memory management and its concepts followed by the implementation of features such as alloc, dealloc, and autorelease.

Reference Counted Memory Management Overview

In many cases in Objective-C, we can rephrase "memory management" as "reference counting." Memory management means that a programmer allocates a memory area when the program needs it and frees it when the program no longer needs it. Unneeded memory areas that are not freed properly are a waste of resources. Also it may crash the application. Reference counting, invented by George E. Collins in 1960, is used to make memory management simple.

To illustrate what reference counting is let's use the following light in an office analogy (Figure 1–1).

On   Off

When someone comes into the office,   When he leaves the office,
he needs the light   he doesn't need it

Figure 1–1. *A lamp in an office*

Imagine that there is only one light in an office. In the morning, when someone comes into the office, he turns on the light because he needs it. When he leaves the office, he does not need it anymore so he turns it off. What will happen if more than one person turns it on and off when they move in and out? Whenever he leaves, he just turns off the light, which means it becomes dark even though others still work there (Figure 1–2).

Figure 1–2. *Problem of light*

To solve this problem, we need some rules to ensure that the light is on when one or more person is there and off only when no one is there.

1. When someone comes into an empty office, she turns on the light.

2. Any following people entering the room use the light as well.

3. When someone leaves, that person no longer needs the light.

4. When the last person leaves, he turns the light off.

For these rules, we introduce a counter to know how many persons there are. Let's see how it works.

1. When someone comes into an empty office, the counter is +1. It becomes one from zero. So the light turns on.

2. When another person comes in, the counter is +1; for instance, it becomes two from one.

3. When someone leaves, the counter is –1; for instance, it becomes one from two.

4. When the last person leaves, the counter becomes zero so the light turns off.

As shown in Figure 1–3, with the counter we can control the light properly. The light is off only when everyone is out.

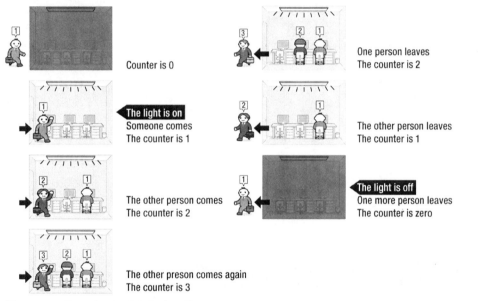

Figure 1–3. *Managing the light in the office*

Let's see how this metaphor helps us to understand memory management. In Objective-C, the light corresponds to an object. Although the office has only one light, in Objective-C we can have many objects up to the limit of the computer's resources.

Each person corresponds to each context of Objective-C. Context is used for a bunch of program code, a variable, a variable scope, or an object. It means something handling a target object. Table 1–1 highlights the relationship of the office light and an object in Objective-C.

Table 1–1. *Comparison of actions for an office lamp and an Objective-C object*

Action for a Lamp	Action for an Objective-C Object
Turn it on	Create an object and have ownership of it
Use it	Take ownership of the object
Not Use it	Relinquish ownership of the object
Turn it off	Discard the object

As we can manage the light with a counter, we can manage application memory in Objective-C. In other words, we can manage objects of Objective-C with reference counting, as shown in Figure 1–4.

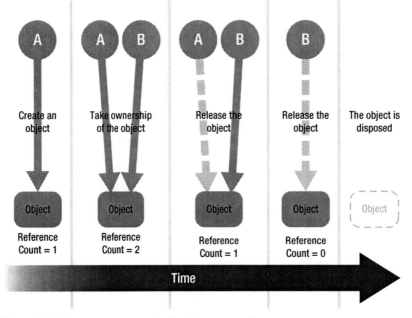

Figure 1–4. *Memory management with reference counting*

This figure illustrates the concept of memory management with reference counting. In the following sections, we dig deeper into this concept and give some examples.

Exploring Memory Management Further

With reference counting, you may think that you need to remember the value of the reference counter itself or what refers to the object, and so on. But you shouldn't. Instead, you should think about reference counting as in the following rules.

▓ You have ownership of any objects you create.

▓ You can take ownership of an object using retain.

▓ When no longer needed, you must relinquish ownership of an object you own.

▓ You must not relinquish ownership of an object you don't own.

Above are all the rules about reference counting. All you have to do is just follow the rules. You don't need to worry any more about the reference counter.

"Create", "take ownership," and "relinquish ownership" in the rules, and "dispose" are very common phrases for reference counting. Table 1–2 shows how these phrases correspond to Objective-C methods.

Table 1–2. *Comparison of actions for Objective-C object and methods*

Action for Objective-C Object	Objective-C Method
Create and have ownership of it	alloc/new/copy/mutableCopy group
Take ownership of it	retain
Relinquish it	release
Dispose of it	dealloc

Basically, you alloc an object, retain it at some point, and then send one release for each alloc/retain you sent. The dealloc method is called on an object when it is being removed from memory.

> **NOTE:** If you used alloc once and then retain once, you need to release twice.

These methods are not provided by the Objective-C language itself. These are features of the Foundation Framework as part of the Cocoa Framework. In the Foundation Framework, NSObject has a class method alloc, and instance methods retain, release, and dealloc to handle memory management (Figure 1–5). Just how this is accomplished is shown later in the "Implementing alloc, retain, release, and dealloc" section.

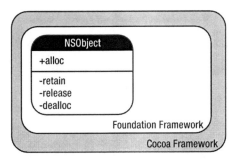

Figure 1–5. *Relationship of Cocoa Framework, Foundation Framework, and NSObject class*

Let's study each rule one by one.

You Have Ownership of Any Objects You Create

You use a method whose name begins with one of the following, which means that you are creating an object and have ownership of it.

- alloc
- new
- copy
- mutableCopy

Let's see how to create an object with some example source code. The following example uses the alloc method to create and have ownership of an object.

```
/*
 * You create an object and have ownership.
 */

id obj = [[NSObject alloc] init];

/*
 * Now, you have ownership of the object.
 */
```

By calling the NSObject class method alloc, you create an object and take ownership of it. The variable obj has a pointer to the created object. You can also create it by using class method new. [NSObject new] and [[NSObject alloc] init] do exactly the same thing.

```
/*
 * You create an object and have ownership.
 */

id obj = [NSObject new];

/*
 * Now you have ownership of the object.
 */
```

NSObject instance method "copy" creates a copy of an object, the class of which has to adopt the NSCopying protocol and copyWithZone: has to be implemented properly. Likewise, the NSObject instance method "mutableCopy" creates a mutable copy of an object, the class of which has to adopt the NSMutableCopying protocol and mutableCopyWithZone: has to be implemented properly. The difference between copy and mutableCopy is like that of NSArray and NSMutableArray. These methods create a new object in the same way as alloc and new do; therefore, you have ownership of it.

As previously described, when you use methods whose name begins with alloc, new, copy, or mutableCopy, you create an object and have ownership. Following are examples of method names.

- allocMyObject

- newThatObject

- copyThis

- mutableCopyYourObject

However, the naming convention is not applied to the following methods.

- allocate

- newer

- copying

- mutableCopyed

> **NOTE:** Please use CamelCase for method names. CamelCase is the practice of writing compound words or phrases in which the elements are joined without spaces, with each element's initial letter capitalized within the compound. For method names, the first letter should be lowercase as in camelCase. See Wikipedia, "CamelCase" http://en.wikipedia.org/wiki/CamelCase

You Can Take Ownership of an Object Using retain

Sometimes methods that are not in the alloc/new/copy/mutableCopy method group return an object. In this case, you haven't created it, so you don't have ownership of it. The following is an example with the NSMutableArray class method array.

```
/*
 * Obtain an object without creating it yourself or having ownership
 */

id obj = [NSMutableArray array];

/*
 * The obtained object exists and you don't have ownership of it.
 */
```

The variable obj has a reference to the NSMutableArray object, but you don't have ownership of it. To take ownership, you have to use the retain method.

```
/*
 * Obtain an object without creating it yourself or having ownership
 */

id obj = [NSMutableArray array];

/*
 * The obtained object exists and you don't have ownership of it.
 */

[obj retain];

/*
 * Now you have ownership of it.
 */
```

After calling the "retain" method, you have ownership of the object as if you had obtained the object with the alloc/new/copy/mutableCopy method group.

When No Longer Needed, You Must Relinquish Ownership of an Object You Own

When you own an object, but don't need it anymore, you must relinquish ownership by calling the release method.

```
/*
 * You create an object and have ownership.
 */

id obj = [[NSObject alloc] init];

/*
 * Now you have ownership of the object.
 */

[obj release];

/*
 * The object is relinquished.
 *
 * Though the variable obj has the pointer to the object,
 * you can't access the object anymore.
 */
```

In the above example, after an object is created and the ownership is taken by alloc, you relinquished it by the release method. You can do the same thing for retained objects as follows.

Relinquishing Ownership of a Retained Object

```
/*
 * Obtain an object without creating it yourself or having ownership
 */

id obj = [NSMutableArray array];

/*
 * The obtained object exists and you don't have ownership of it.
 */

[obj retain];

/*
 * Now you have ownership of the object.
 */

[obj release];

/*
 *  The object is relinquished.
 * You can't access the object anymore.
 */
```

You have to relinquish ownership with the release method when you have ownership of an object for both of these cases: you have created an object and have ownership by calling the alloc/new/copy/mutableCopy method group, or you have ownership by calling the retain method.

Next, let's see how a method can return a created object .

Relinquishing Ownership of a Retained Object

The following example shows how a method can return a created object.

```
- (id)allocObject
{
    /*
     * You create an object and have ownership.
     */

    id obj = [[NSObject alloc] init];

    /*
     * At this moment, this method has ownership of the object.
     */

    return obj;
}
```

If a method returns an object of which the method has ownership, ownership is passed to the caller. Also, please note that in order to be in the alloc/new/copy/mutableCopy method group, the method name must begin with alloc.

```
/*
 * Obtain an object without creating it yourself or having ownership
 */

id obj1 = [obj0 allocObject];

/*
 * Now you have ownership of the object.
 */
```

You call the allocObject method, which means you create an object and have ownership because the method name begins with alloc.

Next, let's see how we can implement a method such as [NSMutableArray array].

Returning a New Object Without Ownership

[NSMutableArray array] method returns a new object without ownership taken by the caller. Let's see how we can implement this kind of method.

We can't declare this kind of method with a name beginning with alloc/new/copy/mutableCopy. In the following example, we use "object" for the method name.

```
- (id)object
{
    id obj = [[NSObject alloc] init];

    /*
     * At this moment, this method has ownership of the object.
     */

    [obj autorelease];

    /*
     * The object exists, and you don't have ownership of it.
     */

    return obj;
}
```

To implement such methods, we use the autorelease method as above (see Figure 1–6). By calling autorelease, you can return the created object without ownership. Autorelease offers a mechanism to relinquish objects properly when the lifetime of the objects has ended.

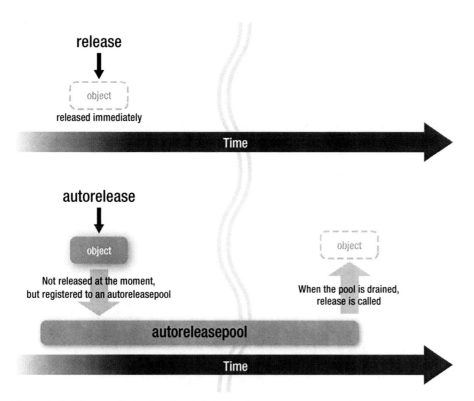

Figure 1–6. *Difference between release and autorelease*

For example, the class method of NSMutableArray, "array" is implemented like this. Please note that in accordance with the naming rule the method name doesn't begin with alloc/new/copy/mutableCopy

```
id obj1 = [obj0 object];

 /*
  * The obtained object exists and you don't have ownership of it.
  */
```

You can take ownership of the autoreleased object by the retain method.

```
id obj1 = [obj0 object];
 /*
  * The obtained object exists and you don't have ownership of it.
  */

[obj1 retain];

 /*
  * Now you have ownership of the object.
  */
```

I explain more autorelease details in a later section.

You Must Not Relinquish Ownership of an Object You Don't Own

As previously described, when you have ownership of objects, you must relinquish them by calling the release method. However, you must not call the release method when you've obtained the object in some other way. If you do, the application will crash. For example, after releasing an object of which you have ownership, if you release it again, the application will crash.

```
/*
 * You create an object and have ownership.
 */

id obj = [[NSObject alloc] init];

/*
 * Now you have ownership of the object.
 */

[obj release];

/*
 * Object is relinquished.
 */

[obj release];

/*
 * You relinquished the object, of which you don't have ownership!
 * The application will crash!
 *
 *   The applications will crash in these cases:
 *   When you call the release method to an already-disposed-of object.
 *   When you access an already-disposed-of object.
 */
```

Also, the following is an example of releasing an object of which you don't have ownership.

```
id obj1 = [obj0 object];

/*
 * The obtained object exists and you don't have ownership of it.
 */

[obj1 release];

/*
 * You relinquished the object of which you don't have ownership!
 * The application will crash sooner or later.
 */
```

As in these examples, you must not relinquish any objects of which you don't have ownership. It causes the application to crash.

We've learned four rules, which are all that you have to consider for memory management with reference counting. Next, we learn how alloc, retain, release, and dealloc are implemented and how they work.

Implementing alloc, retain, release, and dealloc

Many parts of OS X and iOS are publicly available as open source software at Apple Open Source.[1] As mentioned above, the alloc, retain, release, and dealloc are methods of the NSObject class.within the Foundation Framework, as part of the Cocoa Framework, Unfortunately, the Foundation Framework is not a part of Apple Open Source. Fortunately, because the Core Foundation Framework is a part of Apple Open Source, the source code for memory management that is used from NSObject is public. But still, without having the implementation of NSObject itself, it is hard to see the whole picture. So let's check an alternative source code from GNUstep.[2]

GNUstep is a compatible implementation with the Cocoa Framework. Although we can't expect it to be exactly the same as Apple's implementation, it works in the same manner and the implementation should be similar. Understanding GNUstep source code helps us guess Apple's Cocoa implementation.

The alloc Method

Let's start with the alloc method of the NSObject class in GNUstep. As a side note, some source codes in this book might be modified to make the important part clear.

The "alloc" method of the NSObject class is called as in:

```
id obj = [NSObject alloc];
```

The implementation of alloc in NSObject.m is shown in Listing 1–1.

Listing 1–1. *GNUstep/modules/core/base/Source/NSObject.m alloc*

```
+ (id) alloc
{
    return [self allocWithZone: NSDefaultMallocZone()];
}

+ (id) allocWithZone: (NSZone*)z
{
    return NSAllocateObject (self, 0, z);
}
```

Inside the allocWithZone: method, an object is allocated with the NSAllocateObject function. The implementation is shown in Listing 1–2.

---

[1] Apple, "Apple open source," http://opensource.apple.com/

[2] GNUstep, "GNUstep.org," http://gnustep.org/

Listing 1–2. *GNUstep/Modules/Core/Base/Source/NSObject.m NSAllocateObject*

```
struct obj_layout {
    NSUInteger  retained;
};

inline id
NSAllocateObject (Class aClass, NSUInteger extraBytes, NSZone *zone)
{
    int size = /* needed size to store the object */
    id new = NSZoneMalloc(zone, size);
    memset(new, 0, size);
    new = (id)&((struct obj_layout *)new)[1];
}
```

The NSAllocateObject function calls NSZoneMalloc to allocate a memory area. After that, the area is filled with zero and the area pointer is returned.

> **NOTE:** Originally, NSZone was used to prevent memory fragmentation (Figure 1–7). By switching zones case by case, memory allocation could be more effective.
>
> But nowadays, Objective-C runtime just ignores zones as you can see at "Transition to ARC Release Notes."[3] Because a recent runtime memory management algorithm is effective enough, using zones is not considered meaningful or worthwhile because of the complexity.

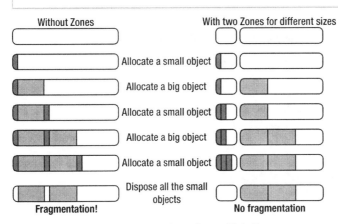

Figure 1–7. *Preventing fragmentation using multiple Zones.*

By removing NSZone-related code, the alloc method can be simply rewritten as in Listing 1–3.

---

[3] Apple, "Transition to ARC Release Notes.", http://developer.apple.com/library/mac/ #releasenotes/ObjectiveC/RN-TransitioningToARC/_index.html

Listing 1–3. *GNUstep/modules/core/base/Source/NSObject.m alloc simplified*

```
struct obj_layout {
    NSUInteger  retained;
};

+ (id) alloc
{
    int size = sizeof(struct obj_layout) + size_of_the_object;
    struct obj_layout *p = (struct obj_layout *)calloc(1, size);
    return (id)(p + 1);
}
```

Now that you understand how the alloc method works, let's move on to retain.

The retain Method

The alloc method returns a memory block filled with zero containing a struct obj_layout header, which has a variable "retained" to store the number of references. This number is called the reference count. Figure 1–8 shows the structure of an object in the GNUstep implementation.

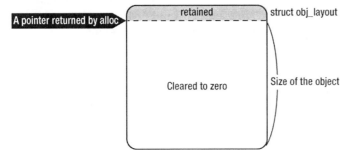

Figure 1–8. *Memory image of an object returned by alloc*

You can get the reference count value by calling the retainCount method.

```
id obj = [[NSObject alloc] init];
NSLog(@"retainCount=%d", [obj retainCount]);

/*
 * retainCount=1 is displayed.
 */
```

Just after alloc is called, the reference count is one. The next source code shows how the retainCount function is implemented in GNUstep.

Listing 1–4. *GNUstep/Modules/Core/Base/Source/NSObject.m retainCount*

```
- (NSUInteger) retainCount
{
    return NSExtraRefCount(self) + 1;
}

inline NSUInteger
NSExtraRefCount(id anObject)
```

```
{
    return ((struct obj_layout *)anObject)[-1].retained;
}
```

The source code searches the header from the object pointer and gets the value of the retained variable (Figure 1–9).

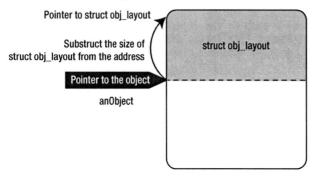

Figure 1–9. *Accessing the header from an object*

Because the memory block is filled with zero when it is allocated, the value of "retained" is zero. The retainCount function returns 1 by "NSExtraRefCount(self) + 1". We can guess that the "retain" or "release" method would modify the value by +1 or –1.

```
[obj retain];
```

Let's check the implementation of the "retain" method, as in Listing 1–5.

Listing 1–5. *GNUstep/Modules/Core/Base/Source/NSObject.m retain*

```
- (id) retain
{
    NSIncrementExtraRefCount(self);
    return self;
}

inline void
NSIncrementExtraRefCount(id anObject)
{
    if (((struct obj_layout *)anObject)[-1].retained == UINT_MAX - 1)
        [NSException raise: NSInternalInconsistencyException
            format: @"NSIncrementExtraRefCount() asked to increment too far"];

    ((struct obj_layout *)anObject)[-1].retained++;
}
```

Although it has a few lines of code to throw an exception, when the variable "retained" overflows, it is fundamentally incremented by one on the line "retained++". Next, we learn the "release" method the functionality of which is opposite to the "retained" method.

The release Method

We can easily guess that the "release" method would have "retained--". Also, it should have some codes when the value becomes zero.

```
[obj release];
```

The "release" method is implemented as shown in Listing 1–6.

Listing 1–6. *GNUstep/Modules/Core/Base/Source/NSObject.m release*

```
- (void) release
{
    if (NSDecrementExtraRefCountWasZero(self))
    [self dealloc];
}

BOOL
NSDecrementExtraRefCountWasZero(id anObject)
{
    if (((struct obj_layout *)anObject)[-1].retained == 0) {
        return YES;
    } else {
        ((struct obj_layout *)anObject)[-1].retained--;
        return NO;
    }
}
```

As we expected, "retained" is decremented by one. If the value is zero, the object will be disposed of by the "dealloc" method. Let's see how the "dealloc" method is implemented.

The dealloc Method

Listing 1–7 is the implementation of the "dealloc" method.

Listing 1–7. *GNUstep/Modules/Core/Base/Source/NSObject.m dealloc*

```
- (void) dealloc
{
    NSDeallocateObject (self);
}

inline void
NSDeallocateObject(id anObject)
{
    struct obj_layout *o = &((struct obj_layout *)anObject)[-1];
    free(o);
}
```

It just disposes of a memory block.

We have seen the implementation of alloc, retain, release, and dealloc in GNUstep and have learned the following.

- All Objective-C objects have an integer value called the reference count.

- The reference count is incremented by one when one of alloc/new/copy/mutableCopy or retain is called.

- It is decremented by one when release is called.

- Dealloc is called when the integer counter becomes zero.

Next, let's check the implementation by Apple.

Apple's Implementation of alloc, retain, release, and dealloc

As I said earlier, the source code of the NSObject class itself is not publicly available. We investigate how the implementation works using an Xcode debugger (lldb) for iOS application. First, set a breakpoint at the NSObject class method alloc. See what happens on the debugger. The following is the list of functions called inside alloc.

```
+alloc
+allocWithZone:
class_createInstance
calloc
```

The NSObject class method alloc calls allocWithZone. After that, through the class_createInstance function, which is documented in the Objective-C Runtime reference, the calloc function is called to allocate the memory block.[4] There does not seem to be much difference with the implementation of GNUstep. We can see the source code of class_createInstance function in objc4 library runtime/objc-runtime-new.mm. [5]

How about NSObject instance methods retainCount, retain, and release? The following functions are called inside.

```
-retainCount
__CFDoExternRefOperation
 CFBasicHashGetCountOfKey
```

```
-retain
__CFDoExternRefOperation
CFBasicHashAddValue
```

---

[4] Apple, "Objective-C Runtime Reference," http://developer.apple.com/library/mac/#documentation/Cocoa/Reference/ObjCRuntimeRef/Reference/reference.html

[5] Apple, "Source Browser," http://www.opensource.apple.com/source/objc4/

```
-release
__CFDoExternRefOperation
CFBasicHashRemoveValue
```

(Also, -dealloc will be called as well when CFBasicHashRemoveValue returns 0.)

In all the above methods, the __CFDoExternRefOperation function is called. Then the function calls similarly named functions. These functions are public. As you can see, if the function names begin with CF, you can find the source codes in the Core Foundation Framework. [6] The source code in Listing 1–8 is the simplified __CFDoExternRefOperation implementation in CFRuntime.c.

Listing 1–8. *CF/CFRuntime.c __CFDoExternRefOperation*

```
int __CFDoExternRefOperation(uintptr_t op, id obj) {
    CFBasicHashRef table = get hashtable from obj;
    int count;

    switch (op) {
    case OPERATION_retainCount:
        count = CFBasicHashGetCountOfKey(table, obj);
        return count;

    case OPERATION_retain:
        CFBasicHashAddValue(table, obj);
        return obj;

    case OPERATION_release:
        count = CFBasicHashRemoveValue(table, obj);
        return 0 == count;
    }
}
```

__CFDoExternRefOperation function is a dispatcher, which calls different functions for retainCount, retain, or release. We can guess these methods would be as follows.

```
- (NSUInteger) retainCount
{
    return (NSUInteger)__CFDoExternRefOperation(OPERATION_retainCount, self);
}

- (id) retain
{
    return (id)__CFDoExternRefOperation(OPERATION_retain, self);
}

- (void) release
{
    return __CFDoExternRefOperation(OPERATION_release, self);
}
```

---

[6] Apple, "Source Browser", http://www.opensource.apple.com/source/CF/

As you can see in the __CFDoExternRefOperation function above, Apple's implementation seems to handle the reference count by a hash table (reference counter table) as shown in Figure 1–10.

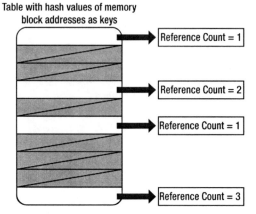

Figure 1–10. *Managing Reference Counts with a hash table*

In the GNUstep implementation, reference counts are in the header of each object's memory block. But in Apple's implementation, all the reference counts are stored in entries of a hash table. Although GNUstep implementation looks simpler and faster, there might be some merit to Apple's as well.

Here are the benefits if reference counts are stored in each object's header as in GNUstep's implementation:

- Fewer codes.

- It is quite simple to manage the lifetime, because each memory area of the reference count itself is included in the object memory area.

How about if reference counts are stored in a hash table as in Apple's?

- Each object doesn't have a header, thus there is no need to worry about alignment issues for the header area.

- By iterating through the hash table entries, memory blocks for each object are reachable.

The latter is especially useful for debugging. When the memory area of some objects is broken and the table is still there, the debugger can reach the objects' pointers (Figure 1–11).

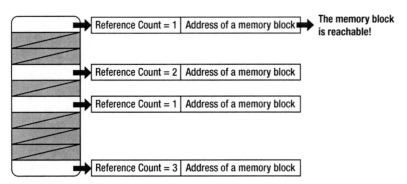

Figure 1–11. *Finding objects in the Reference Count table*

Also, to detect memory leaks, instruments check the entries of the table and determine whether someone has ownership of each object.

That's it for Apple's implementation. Now that we have a better understanding of how Apple has implemented things, there is one more item to learn regarding memory management in Objective-C: autorelease.

Autorelease

Because of its name, you might think that autorelease is something like ARC. But it is not. It is more like "automatic variable" in the C language.[7]

Let's start by reviewing what automatic variable is in C. We then look at the source code of GNUstep to understand how autorelease works, followed by Apple's implementation of autorelease.

Automatic Variables

An *automatic variable* is a lexically scoped variable, which is disposed of automatically when the execution leaves the scope.

```
{
    int a;
}

/*
 * Because the variable scope is left,
 * auto variable 'int a' is disposed of and can't be accessed anymore.
 */
```

With autorelease, you can use objects in the same manner as automatic variables, meaning that when execution leaves a code block, the "release" method is called on the object automatically. You can control the block itself as well.

---

[7] Wikipedia, "Automatic Variable," http://en.wikipedia.org/wiki/Automatic_variable

The following steps and Figure 1–12 show you how to use the "autorelease" instance method.

1. Create an NSAutoreleasePool object.

2. Call "autorelease" to allocated objects.

3. Discard the NSAutoreleasePool object.

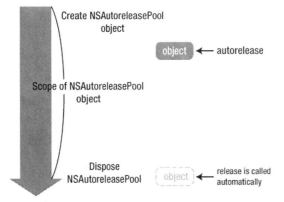

Figure 1–12. *Lifetime of an NSAutoreleasePool object*

A code block between the creation and disposal of the NSAutoreleasePool object is equivalent to the variable scope in C. When an NSAutoreleasePool object is disposed of, the release method is automatically called for all the autoreleased objects. Some example source code is as follows.

```
NSAutoreleasePool *pool = [[NSAutoreleasePool alloc] init];
id obj = [[NSObject alloc] init];
[obj autorelease];
[pool drain];
```

In the last line of the above source code, [pool drain] will do [obj release].

In the Cocoa Framework, NSAutoreleasePool objects are created, owned, or disposed of all over the place, such as NSRunLoop, which is the main loop of the application (Figure 1–13). So, you don't need to use the NSAutoreleasePool object explicitly.

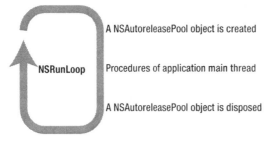

Figure 1–13. *A NSAutoreleasePool object is created and disposed of each time in NSRunLoop.*

But when there are too many autoreleased objects, application memory becomes short (Figure 1–14). It happens because the objects still exist until the NSAutoreleasePool object is discarded. A typical example of this is loading and resizing many images. Many autoreleased objects, such as NSData objects for reading files, UImage objects for the data, and resized images exist at the same time.

```
for (int i = 0; i < numberOfImages; ++i) {
    /*
     * Processing images, such as loading,etc.
     * Too many autoreleased objects exist,
     * because NSAutoreleasePool object is not discarded.
     * At some point, it causes memory shortage.
     */
}
```

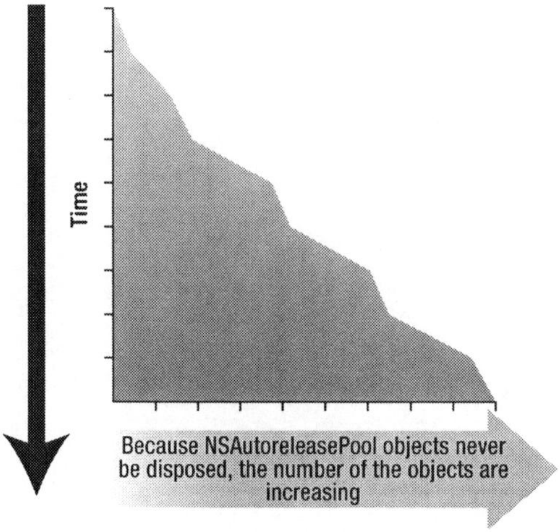

Figure 1–14. *The increasing number of autoreleased objects*

In this case, you should create and discard an NSAutoreleasePool object by yourself explicitly at the appropriate time (Figure 1–15).

```
for (int i = 0; i < numberOfImages; ++i) {
    NSAutoreleasePool *pool = [[NSAutoreleasePool alloc] init];

    /*
     * Loading images, etc.
     * Too many autoreleased objects exist.
     */

    [pool drain];

    /*
     * All the autoreleased objects are released by [pool drain].
     */
}
```

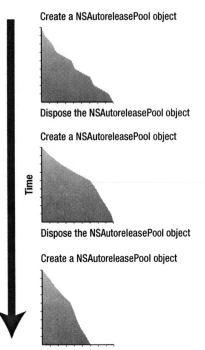

Create a NSAutoreleasePool object

Dispose the NSAutoreleasePool object

Create a NSAutoreleasePool object

Dispose the NSAutoreleasePool object

Create a NSAutoreleasePool object

Dispose the NSAutoreleasePool object

Figure 1–15. *Autoreleased object should be properly released.*

With the Cocoa Framework, you will see many class methods returning autoreleased objects, such as the "arrayWithCapacity" method of the NSMutableArray class.

```
id array = [NSMutableArray arrayWithCapacity:1];
```

The above source code is equivalent to:

```
id array = [[[NSMutableArray alloc] initWithCapacity:1] autorelease];
```

Implementing autorelease

In this section, we discuss the implementation of autorelease in GNUstep as we did for alloc, retain, release, and dealloc to learn how it works in detail.

```
[obj autorelease];
```

This source code calls the NSObject instance method "autorelease". Listing 1–9 shows the implementation of the autorelease method.

Listing 1–9. *GNUstep/Modules/Core/Base/Source/NSObject.m autorelease*

```
- (id) autorelease
{
    [NSAutoreleasePool addObject:self];
}
```

Actually, autorelease just calls the NSAutoreleasePool class method addObject. In GNUstep, it is implemented bit different. But this is just for optimization as you can see below.

OPTIMIZATION ON OBJECTIVE-C METHOD CALL

In GNUstep, the autorelease method is implemented in an irregular way for optimization purposes. Because autorelease is called so often in iOS and OSX applications, it has a special mechanism called IMP caching. When the framework is initialized, it caches some search results, such as function pointers and name resolution of classes and methods. If the mechanism doesn't exist, these procedures have to be done when autorelease is called.

```
id autorelease_class = [NSAutoreleasePool class];
SEL autorelease_sel = @selector(addObject:);
IMP autorelease_imp = [autorelease_class methodForSelector: autorelease_sel];
```

When the method is called, it just returns a cached value.

```
- (id) autorelease
{
    (*autorelease_imp)(autorelease_class, autorelease_sel, self);
}
```

Above is the method call with IMP caching. It can be rewritten as follows if IMP caching is not there. It is about two times faster with the caching mechanism though, depending on the environment.

```
- (id) autorelease
{
    [NSAutoreleasePool addObject:self];
}
```

Let's see the implementation of the NSAutoreleasePool class. Listing 1–10 is a simplified source code in NSAutoreleasePool.

Listing 1–10. *GNUstep/Modules/Core/Base/Source/NSAutoreleasePool.m addObject*

```
+ (void) addObject: (id)anObj
{
    NSAutoreleasePool *pool = getting active NSAutoreleasePool;
    if (pool != nil) {
        [pool addObject:anObj];
    } else {
        NSLog(@"autorelease is called without active NSAutoreleasePool.");
    }
}
```

The Class method "addObject" calls NSAutoreleasePool instance method "addObject" for the active NSAutoreleasePool object. In the next example, a variable "pool" is the active NSAutoreleasePool object.

```
NSAutoreleasePool *pool = [[NSAutoreleasePool alloc] init];
id obj = [[NSObject alloc] init];
[obj autorelease];
```

When multiple NSAutoreleasePool objects are created and nested, the innermost object becomes active. In the next example, pool2 is active.

```
NSAutoreleasePool *pool0 = [[NSAutoreleasePool alloc] init];

    NSAutoreleasePool *pool1 = [[NSAutoreleasePool alloc] init];

        NSAutoreleasePool *pool2 = [[NSAutoreleasePool alloc] init];

        id obj = [[NSObject alloc] init];
        [obj autorelease];

        [pool2 drain];

    [pool1 drain];

[pool0 drain];
```

Next, let's take a look at the implementation of the NSAutoreleasePool instance method addObject as well (Listing 1–11).

Listing 1–11. *GNUstep/Modules/Core/Base/Source/NSAutoreleasePool.m addObject*

```
- (void) addObject: (id)anObj
{
    [array addObject:anObj];
}
```

It adds the object to a mutable array. In the original GNUstep implementation, linked list is used instead of array. Anyway, the object is stored in a container, which means that when the instance method "autorelease" of NSObject is called, the object is added to the container in an active NSAutoreleasePool object.

```
[pool drain];
```

Next, let's see how the active NSAutoreleasePool object is disposed of when drain is called (Listing 1–12).

Listing 1–12. *GNUstep/Modules/Core/Base/Source/NSAutoreleasePool.m drain*

```
- (void) drain
{
    [self dealloc];
}

- (void) dealloc
{
    [self emptyPool];
    [array release];
}

- (void) emptyPool
{
    for (id obj in array) {
        [obj release];
    }
}
```

We can see that the "release" method is called for all the objects in the pool.

Apple's Implementation of autorelease

We can see Apple's implementation of autorelease in runtime/objc-arr.mm in the objc4 library. The source code is shown in Listing 1–13.

Listing 1–13. *objc4/runtime/objc-arr.mm class AutoreleasePoolPage*

```
class AutoreleasePoolPage
{
    static inline void *push()
    {
        /* It corresponds to creation and ownership of an NSAutoreleasePool object */
    }

    static inline void pop(void *token)
    {
        /* It corresponds to disposal of an NSAutoreleasePool object */
        releaseAll();
    }

    static inline id autorelease(id obj)
    {
        /* It corresponds to NSAutoreleasePool class method addObject. */
        AutoreleasePoolPage *autoreleasePoolPage = /* getting active AutoreleasePoolPage
object */
        autoreleasePoolPage->add(obj);
    }

    id *add(id obj)
    {
        /* add the obj to an internal array; */
    }

    void releaseAll()
    {
        /* calls release for all the objects in the internal array */
    }
};

void *objc_autoreleasePoolPush(void)
{
    return AutoreleasePoolPage::push();
}

void objc_autoreleasePoolPop(void *ctxt)
{
    AutoreleasePoolPage::pop(ctxt);
}

id objc_autorelease(id obj)
{
    return AutoreleasePoolPage::autorelease(obj);
}
```

The functions and the AutoreleasePoolPage class are implemented using a C++ class and a dynamic array. The functions seem to work the same as in GNUstep. As we did previously with the debugger, we investigate what functions are called in the autorelease and NSAutoreleasePool class methods. These methods will call objc4 functions, which are related to autorelease:

```
NSAutoreleasePool *pool = [[NSAutoreleasePool alloc] init];
/* equivalent to objc_autoreleasePoolPush() */

id obj = [[NSObject alloc] init];

[obj autorelease];
/* equivalent to objc_autorelease(obj)  */

[pool drain];
/* equivalent to objc_autoreleasePoolPop(pool) */
```

By the way, in iOS, the NSAutoreleasePool class has a method to check the status of autoreleased objects. The method, showPools, displays the current status of NSAutoreleasePool to the console. It can be used only for debugging purposes because it is a private method. You can use it as

```
[NSAutoreleasePool showPools];
```

With the latest Objective-C runtime, instead of the "showPools" method, _objc_autoreleasePoolPrint() is provided because "showPools" works in iOS only, This method is also a private method so you can use it for debugging purposes only.

```
/* declare function */
extern void _objc_autoreleasePoolPrint();

/* display autoreleasepool status for debug. */
_objc_autoreleasePoolPrint();
```

Then you can see the status of AutoreleasePoolPage. The result is as follows.

```
objc[14481]: ##############
objc[14481]: AUTORELEASE POOLS for thread 0xad0892c0
objc[14481]: 14 releases pending.
objc[14481]: [0x6a85000]  ...............  PAGE  (hot) (cold)
objc[14481]: [0x6a85028]  ###############  POOL 0x6a85028
objc[14481]: [0x6a8502c]          0x6719e40  __NSCFString
objc[14481]: [0x6a85030]  ###############  POOL 0x6a85030
objc[14481]: [0x6a85034]          0x7608100  __NSArrayI
objc[14481]: [0x6a85038]          0x7609a60  __NSCFData
objc[14481]: [0x6a8503c]  ###############  POOL 0x6a8503c
objc[14481]: [0x6a85040]          0x8808df0  __NSCFDictionary
objc[14481]: [0x6a85044]          0x760ab50  NSConcreteValue
objc[14481]: [0x6a85048]          0x760afe0  NSConcreteValue
objc[14481]: [0x6a8504c]          0x760b280  NSConcreteValue
objc[14481]: [0x6a85050]          0x760b2f0  __NSCFNumber
objc[14481]: [0x6a851a8]  ###############  POOL 0x6a851a8
objc[14481]: [0x6a851ac]          0x741d1e0  Test
objc[14481]: [0x6a851b0]          0x671c660  NSObject
objc[14481]: ##############
```

It is very useful to know if some objects are autoreleased or not, as noted in the following sidebar.

AUTORELEASE NSAUTORELEASEPOOL OBJECT

Question: What will happen if "autorelease" is called on an NSAutoreleasePool object?

```
NSAutoreleasePool *pool = [[NSAutoreleasePool alloc] init];
[pool autorelease];
```

Answer: The application will be terminated.

```
*** Terminating app due to uncaught exception 'NSInvalidArgumentException'
reason: '*** -[NSAutoreleasePool autorelease]:
Cannot autorelease an autorelease pool'
```

When autorelease is called in Objective-C with the Foundation framework, an NSObject instance method is called for in almost all the cases. However, the NSAutoreleasePool class overrides autorelease to show an error when autorelease is called on autoreleasepool.

Summary

You've learned the following in this chapter.

- ▧ The concept of memory management with reference counting

- ▧ How alloc, retain ,release, and dealloc methods are implemented

- ▧ The mechanism of autorelease and its implementation

These items are important and still applicable even if ARC is introduced. In the next chapter we learn how the situation will be change

Chapter 2

ARC Rules

In the previous chapter, we reviewed memory management in Objective-C for a non-ARC environment. But what happens when ARC is enabled? This chapter explores the changes incurred when ARC is employed. Automatic Reference Counting was briefly explained in Chapter 1, but it is really best summarized in Apple's own words:

> *Automatic Reference Counting (ARC) in Objective-C makes memory management the job of the compiler. By enabling ARC with the new Apple LLVM compiler, you will never need to type retain or release again, dramatically simplifying the development process, while reducing crashes and memory leaks. The compiler has a complete understanding of your objects, and releases each object the instant it is no longer used, so apps run as fast as ever, with predictable, smooth performance.*[1]

First, we show the relationship of the reference counting rules with ARC, and we also learn the ownership specifiers one by one, which are newly introduced by ARC. Also ARC brings us new properties. And most important, we learn the rules to make your code ARC-friendly: by simply following the rules, you can write code for ARC with confidence.

Overview

Actually, reference counting is still used as the basis of ARC, but ARC helps the reference counting mechanism work automatically when you follow the rules that are explained in this chapter.

In fact, we can enable or disable ARC for each compilable unit. For example, we can enable or disable ARC for each source file as shown in Figure 2–1.

---

[1] Apple, "iOS 5 for developers," http://developer.apple.com/technologies/ios5/

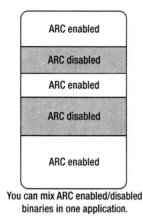

You can mix ARC enabled/disabled
binaries in one application.

Figure 2–1. *Enabling or disabling ARC for each source file in one application*

In summary, the most important part of ARC is that you, the programmer, no longer need to call "retain" or "release." Under the following conditions, your source code will be automatically compiled with ARC enabled:

- clang(LLVM compiler) 3.0 and newer

- Compile option –fobjc-arc

Clang is the default compiler and the –fobjc-arc option is set as the default in Xcode 4.2. Therefore, when you work in Xcode 4.2, you don't need to do anything special.

From here, all the source codes are for an ARC-enabled environment. We have the comment /* non-ARC */ if the source code is for a non-ARC environment. In the next section, we show how the reference counting mechanism is changed when ARC is enabled.

Reference Counting Mechanism Changes

As we described previously, the rules of reference counting are as follows.

- You have ownership of any objects you create.

- You can take ownership of an object using retain.

- When you no longer need it, you must relinquish ownership of an object of which you have ownership.

- You must not relinquish ownership of an object of which you don't have ownership.

Even when ARC is enabled, these rules are still applicable. But you need some modification to source codes. To do so, you first need to understand ownership qualifiers, which are newly introduced for ARC.

Ownership qualifiers

In Objective-C, 'id' or each object type is used for object variable types.

Object types are pointer types of Objective-C classes, such as NSObject *. 'id' type is used to hide its class name. 'id' is equivalent to void* in the C language.

With ARC, 'id' and object type variables must have one of the following four ownership qualifiers:

- ▓ __strong

- ▓ __weak

- ▓ __unsafe_unretained

- ▓ __autoreleasing

You should decide which ownership qualifier is to be used for all the 'id' and object type variables in your source code. In this chapter, I explain how you should choose each qualifier one by one.

__strong ownership qualifier

The __strong ownership qualifier is used as the default for 'id' and object types. It means that the variable obj in the following source code is __strong qualified implicitly.

```
id obj = [[NSObject alloc] init];
```

Without being explicitly qualified, 'id' or objects are treated as __strong. The above code is the same as

```
id __strong obj = [[NSObject alloc] init];
```

The following is the same source code for a non-ARC environment.

```
/* non-ARC */
id obj = [[NSObject alloc] init];
```

There is no difference thus far. Let's see the next example.

```
{
    id __strong obj = [[NSObject alloc] init];
}
```

Local variable scope is added intentionally. The non-ARC version for this source code is:

```
/* non-ARC */
{
```

```
        id obj = [[NSObject alloc] init];
        [obj release];
}
```

This means the "release" method is automatically added on an ARC environment to release the created object with ownership. When the control flow leaves the scope of the variable obj, the release method is called for the variable because the variable obj is qualified with __strong.

As it is named __strong, this ownership qualifier indicates a strong reference for the object. When the control flow leaves the variable scope, the strong reference disappears and the assigned object is released. Let's find ownership status in the source code.

```
{
    id __strong obj = [[NSObject alloc] init];
}
```

This code creates an object and has ownership of it. We add comments on the ownership status.

```
{
    /*
     * You create an object and have ownership.
     */

    id __strong obj = [[NSObject alloc] init];

    /*
     * The variable obj is qualified with __strong.
     * Which means, it has ownership of the object.
     */

}

/*
 * Leaving the scope of variable obj, its strong reference disappears.
 * The object is released automatically.
 * Because no one has ownership, the object is disposed of.
 */
```

Assigning to __strong ownership qualified variables

The ownership and lifetime of the object are very clear. Next, we see what happens when you obtain an object without creating it yourself or having ownership.

```
{
    id __strong obj = [NSMutableArray array];
}
```

It calls the class method "array" of NSMutableArray to obtain an object without creating it yourself or having ownership.

```
{
    /*
     * Obtain an object without creating it yourself or having ownership
     */
```

```
    id __strong obj = [NSMutableArray array];

    /*
     * The variable obj is qualified with __strong.
     * Which means, it has ownership of the object.
     */

}
/*
 * Leaving the scope of variable obj, its strong reference disappears.
 * The object is released automatically.
 */
```

Ownership and lifetime of the object are very clear in this case as well. And, of course, you can exchange values between variables qualified with __strong as follows.

```
id __strong obj0 = [[NSObject alloc] init];
id __strong obj1 = [[NSObject alloc] init];
id __strong obj2 = nil;
obj0 = obj1;
obj2 = obj0;
obj1 = nil;

obj0 = nil;
obj2 = nil;
```

How the strong reference works

We investigate the example with comments to understand how the strong reference works as in Listing 2–1.

Listing 2–1. *How the strong reference works*

```
id __strong obj0 = [[NSObject alloc] init];  /* object A */

/*
 * obj0 has a strong reference to object A
 */

id __strong obj1 = [[NSObject alloc] init];  /* object B */

/*
 * obj1 has a strong reference to object B
 */

id __strong obj2 = nil;

/*
 * obj2 has no reference
 */

obj0 = obj1;

/*
 *Obj0 has a strong reference to object B, which has been assigned from obj1.
 * So, obj0 does not have a strong reference to object A anymore.
```

```
  * Object A is disposed of because no one has ownership of it.
  *
  * At this moment, both obj0 and obj1 have strong references to object B.
  */

obj2 = obj0;

 /*
  * Through obj0, obj2 has a strong reference to object B.
  *
  * At this moment, obj0, obj1 and obj2 have strong references to object B.
  */

obj1 = nil;

 /*
  * Because nil is assigned to obj1, strong references to object B disappear.
  *
  * At this moment, obj0 and obj2 have strong references to object B.
  */

obj0 = nil;

 /*
  * Because nil is assigned to obj0, a strong reference to object B disappears.
  *
  * At this moment, obj2 has a strong reference to object B.
  */

obj2 = nil;

 /*
  * Because nil is assigned to obj2, a strong reference to object B disappears.
  * Object B is disposed of because no one has ownership of it
  */
```

As in the example (Listing 2–1), ownership is properly managed not only by variable scope, but also by assignments between variables, which are qualified with __strong. Of course, a __strong qualifier can be used as a member variable of Objective-C class or any argument of methods as in Listing 2–2.

Listing 2–2. _Strong qualifiers for member variable and method's argument_

```
@interface Test : NSObject
{
    id __strong obj_;
}
- (void)setObject:(id __strong)obj;
@end

@implementation Test
- (id)init
{
    self = [super init];
    return self;
}

- (void)setObject:(id __strong)obj
```

```
{
    obj_ = obj;
}
@end
```

Let's see how we can use the class.

```
{
    id __strong test = [[Test alloc] init];
    [test setObject:[[NSObject alloc] init]];
}
```

As usual, let's investigate line by line with some comments (Listing 2–3).

Listing 2–3. _Strong qualifiers for member variable and method's argument with comments

```
{
    id __strong test = [[Test alloc] init];

/*
  * test has a strong reference to a Test Object
  */

[test setObject:[[NSObject alloc] init]];

  /*
   * The member obj_ of the object
   * has a strong reference to a NSObject instance.
   */

}
  /*
   * Leaving the scope of variable test, its strong reference disappears.
   * The Test object is released.
   * It is disposed of because no one has ownership.
   *
   * When it is disposed of,
   * The strong reference by its member obj_ disappears as well.
   * The object of NSObject is released.
   * It is disposed of because no one has ownership as well.
   */
```

As the example above shows, it is very easy to use a __strong ownership qualifier for a class member and an argument of a method. In a later section, I explain how it can be used for a class property.

By the way, any variables that are qualified with __strong, __weak, and __autoreleasing, are initialized with nil. Let's see it with an example.

```
id __strong obj0;
id __weak obj1;
id __autoreleasing obj2;
```

The above source code is equivalent to the following.

```
id __strong obj0 = nil;
id __weak obj1 = nil;
id __autoreleasing obj2 = nil;
```

As we saw earlier, Apple says that you don't need to type retain or release any more. Please note that the following rules for reference counting are still fulfilled.

- You have ownership of any objects you create.

- You can take ownership of an object using retain.

- When you no longer need it, you must relinquish ownership of an object of which you have ownership.

- You must not relinquish ownership of an object of which you don't have ownership.

The first two rules are achieved by assigning to a __strong variable. The third rule is achieved automatically by leaving variable scope, by assigning to variables, or when objects having a member variable are discarded. The last rule is very clear because releases are never typed. So all the rules are still fulfilled.

You don't even need to type __strong because it is the default for 'id' and object types. By just enabling ARC, the rules are fulfilled automatically.

__weak ownership qualifier

It may appear that the compiler can perform memory management with only the __strong ownership qualifier. Unfortunately, that's not the case because one big problem can't be solved: circular reference [Figure 2–2]. The following describes how circular reference occurs.

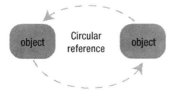

Figure 2–2. *Circular reference*

Circular Reference

Examples in this section show how a circular reference occurs. For instance, it occurs when a member variable of a class has a reference to an object. Assume that we have a class as in Listing 2–4.

Listing 2–4. _A class that may cause circular reference

```
@interface Test : NSObject
{
    id __strong obj_;
}
- (void)setObject:(id __strong)obj;
```

```
@end

@implementation Test
- (id)init
{
    self = [super init];
    return self;
}

- (void)setObject:(id __strong)obj
{
    obj_ = obj;
}
@end
```

We can easily produce a circular reference problem with the class as in Listing 2–5.

Listing 2–5. *Produces circular reference*

```
{
    id test0 = [[Test alloc] init];

    id test1 = [[Test alloc] init];
    [test0 setObject:test1];
    [test1 setObject:test0];
}
```

Adding a few comments opens this example up a little bit (Listing 2–6).

Listing 2–6. *Produces circular reference with comments*

```
{
    id test0 = [[Test alloc] init]; /* object A */

     /*
      * test0 has a strong reference to object A
      */

    id test1 = [[Test alloc] init]; /* object B */

     /*
      * test1 has a strong reference to object B
      */

    [test0 setObject:test1];

     /*
      * The member variable obj_ of object A has a strong reference to object B.
      *
      * At this moment, obj_ of object A and test1 have strong references to object B.
      */

    [test1 setObject:test0];

     /*
      * The member variable obj_ of object B has a strong reference to objectA
      *
      * At this moment, obj_ of object B and test0 have strong references to objectA.
      */
```

```
}
 /*
  * Leaving the scope of variable test0, its strong reference disappears.
  * object A is released automatically.
  *
  * Leaving the scope of variable test1, its strong reference disappears.
  * object B is released automatically.
  *
  * At this moment, obj_ of object B has a strong reference to object A.
  *
  * At this moment, obj_ of object A has a strong reference to object B.
  *
  * memory leaked!!
  */
```

Figure 2–3 illustrates this situation.

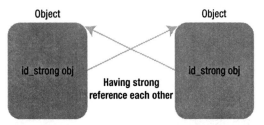

Figure 2–3. *Circular reference with class member variables*

With circular reference, memory leaks happen very often. A memory leak means that some objects still remain in memory even after they are thought to be discarded.

In the example, when the control flow leaves the variable scope of test0 and test1, object A and object B were planned to be discarded. At this point, they should be disposed of because no one has an entry point to the objects. But because of circular reference, they remain.

Self Reference

The next example shows that even one object can produce a circular reference by referencing the object itself. It is sometimes called "self reference" as shown in Figure 2–4.

```
id test = [[Test alloc] init];
[test setObject:test];
```

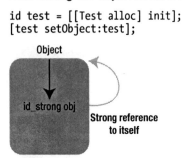

Figure 2–4. *Self reference*

How can we avoid this situation? As we have a __strong ownership qualifier, you might have noticed there is a __weak ownership qualifier. By using a __weak ownership qualifier, we can avoid a circular reference as shown in Figure 2–5.

A __weak ownership qualifier provides a weak reference. A weak reference does not have ownership of the object. Let's see the next example.

```
id __weak obj = [[NSObject alloc] init];
```

The variable obj is qualified with __weak. When the source code is compiled, the compiler shows a warning message.

```
warning: assigning retained obj to weak variable; obj will be
        released after assignment [-Warc-unsafe-retained-assign]
            id __weak obj = [[NSObject alloc] init];
               ^          ~~~~~~~~~~~~~~~~~~~~~~~~~
```

In the example, a created object is assigned to a variable obj, which has been qualified with __weak. So, the variable obj has a weak reference to the object, which means the variable doesn't have ownership. Because no one can take ownership of the created object, the object will be released just after creation. The compiler warns about that case. If you assign the object to a __strong variable at first, the warning will disappear as follows.

```
{
    id __strong obj0 = [[NSObject alloc] init];
    id __weak obj1 = obj0;
}
```

Let's see the source code with comments on ownership status.

```
{
    /*
     * You create an object and have ownership.
     */

    id __strong obj0 = [[NSObject alloc] init];

    /*
     * The variable obj0 is qualified with __strong.
     * Which means, it has ownership of the object.
     */

    id __weak obj1 = obj0;

    /*
     * variable obj1 has a weak reference of the created object
     */

}
    /*
     * Leaving the scope of variable obj0, its strong reference disappears.
     * The object is released automatically.
     * Because no one has ownership, the object is discarded.
     */
```

Because a __weak reference does not have ownership, the object is disposed of when the control flow leaves the variable scope. Now we've learned that we should use the __weak ownership qualifier to avoid cyclic reference. We can rewrite the previous example as follows.

```
@interface Test : NSObject
{
    id __weak obj_;
}
- (void)setObject:(id __strong)obj;
@end
```

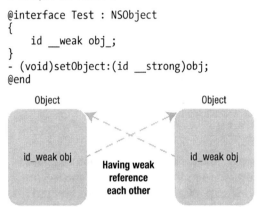

Figure 2–5. *Avoid circular reference with the __weak ownership qualifier*

Weak Reference Disappears

And, there is one more thing you should know about the __weak ownership qualifier. When a variable has a reference to an object and the object is discarded, the weak reference also disappears automatically, which means that the variable is assigned to nil. Let's check it with an example (Listing 2–7).

Listing 2–7. *Weak reference disappears*

```
id __weak obj1 = nil;
{
    id __strong obj0 = [[NSObject alloc] init];

    obj1 = obj0;

    NSLog(@"A: %@", obj1);
}

NSLog(@"B: %@", obj1);
```

The result is:

```
A: <NSObject: 0x753e180>
B: (null)
```

Let's see the source code again with comments on ownership status (Listing 2–8).

Listing 2–8. *Weak reference disappears with comments*

```
id __weak obj1 = nil;

{
    /*
     * You create an object and have ownership.
```

```
        */

    id __strong obj0 = [[NSObject alloc] init];

    /*
     * The variable obj0 is qualified with __strong.
     * Which means, it has ownership of the object.
     */

    obj1 = obj0;

    /*
     * variable obj1 has a weak reference of the object
     */

    NSLog(@"A: %@", obj0);

    /*
     * The object, to which the variable obj0 has a strong reference, is displayed
     */

}
/*
 * Leaving the scope of variable obj0, its strong reference disappears.
 * The object is released.
 * It is disposed of because no one has ownership.
 *
 * When it is disposed of,
 * weak reference is destroyed and nil is assigned to the obj1.
 */

NSLog(@"B: %@", obj1);

/*
 * The value of obj1, nil is displayed
 */
```

With the __weak ownership qualifier, we can avoid cyclic reference. Also by checking if the __weak variable is nil, we can know if the object still exists or is already discarded.

Unfortunately the __weak ownership qualifier is usable only for applications targeting iOS5 (or later) or OSX Lion (or later). For applications targeting older environments, __unsafe_unretained must be used instead.

__unsafe_unretained ownership qualifier

The __unsafe_unretained ownership qualifier is, as the name suggests, absolutely unsafe. Normally, due to ARC, the compiler executes memory management. But any variables qualified with __unsafe_unretained are excluded from the mechanism. So, you have to take care of the variables manually.

```
id __unsafe_unretained obj = [[NSObject alloc] init];
```

This source code is to assign an object to a variable, which is qualified with __unsafe_unretained. The compiler shows the following warning message.

```
warning: assigning retained obj to unsafe_unretained variable;
        obj will be released after assignment [-Warc-unsafe-retained-assign]
    id __unsafe_unretained obj = [[NSObject alloc] init];
                                ^        ~~~~~~~~~~~~~~~~~~~~~~~
```

__unsafe_unretained variables don't have ownership of an object, the same as __weak . In the above example, the object is released just after the object is created. It seems that __unsafe_unretained and __weak qualifier work the same. You will see how __unsafe_unretained is different from __weak in the following (Listing 2–9).

Listing 2–9. *_unsafe_unretained qualifier*

```
id __unsafe_unretained obj1 = nil;

{
    id __strong obj0 = [[NSObject alloc] init];

    obj1 = obj0;

    NSLog(@"A: %@", obj1);
}

NSLog(@"B: %@", obj1);
```

The result is:

```
A: <NSObject: 0x753e180>
B: <NSObject: 0x753e180>
```

Let's see the source code again with comments as usual (Listing 2–10).

Listing 2–10. *_unsafe_unretained qualifier with comments*

```
id __unsafe_unretained obj1 = nil;

{
    /*
     * You create an object and have ownership.
     */

    id __strong obj0 = [[NSObject alloc] init];

    /*
     * The variable obj0 is qualified with __strong.
     * Which means, it has ownership of the object.
     */

    obj1 = obj0;

    /*
     * variable obj1 is assigned from variable obj0,
     * obj1 does not have either strong or weak reference
     */

    NSLog(@"A: %@", obj1);

    /*
     * Display the value of obj1
     */
```

```
}
 /*
  * Leaving the scope of variable obj0, its strong reference disappears.
  * The object is released automatically.
  * Because no one has ownership, the object is discarded.
  */


NSLog(@"B: %@", obj1);

 /*
  * Display the value of obj1
  *
  * The object referenced from obj1 is already discarded.
  * It is called dangling pointer.
  * Invalid access!!
  */
```

Though the last NSLog looks fine, it just works by chance. The application crashes depending on conditions. To assign an object to a variable qualified with __unsafe_unretained, you have to make sure that the object exists and has been assigned to some variables qualified with __strong. I recommend reconsidering the reason why you need __unsafe_unretained. You need to understand why completely; for example, you might need it because the application has to support iOS4 or OS X Snow Leopard and you need to use it instead of __weak. Also, you have to be sure that the assigned object exists during the lifetime of the variable. If it fails, the application will crash and no one will use your application.

__autoreleasing ownership qualifier

Let's see if there are any changes related to autorelease with ARC. To put simply, you can't use the autorelease method. You can't use the NSAutoreleasePool class either. I explain it later with some rules. Although you can't directly use autorelease, there is a mechanism of autorelease still. Without ARC, we've used autorelease as follows.

```
/* non-ARC */

NSAutoreleasePool *pool = [[NSAutoreleasePool alloc] init];

id obj = [[NSObject alloc] init];

[obj autorelease];

[pool drain];
```

This source code can be rewritten for an ARC-enabled environment.

```
@autoreleasepool {

    id __autoreleasing obj = [[NSObject alloc] init];

}
```

Instead of creating, having, and discarding an NSAutoreleasePool class object, you have to enclose codes with @autoreleasepool block. Instead of calling the autorelease method, you have to assign the object to a variable qualified with __autoreleasing. Assigning the object to the __autoreleasing qualified variable is equivalent to calling autorelease on a non-ARC environment. By doing it, the object is registered to an autoreleasepool. So, with ARC enabled, you just have to use @autoreleasepool instead of NSAutoreleasePool class and use the __autoreleasing qualified variable instead of the autorelease method as shown in Figure 2–6.

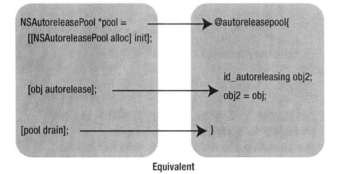

Figure 2–6. *@autoreleasepool and a variable with __autoreleasing qualifier*

But in reality, it is very rare to type __autoreleasing explicitly. Let's see why you don't need to type __autoreleasing very often.

Compiler Cares __autoreleasing Automatically

To obtain an object without creation, you use some methods not in the alloc/new/copy/mutableCopy method group. In this case, the object is automatically registered to the autoreleasepool. It is same as obtaining an autoreleased object. When an object is returned from a method, the compiler checks if the method begins with alloc/new/copy/mutableCopy, and if not, the returned object is automatically registered to the autorelease pool. Exceptionally, any method whose name begins with init, doesn't register the return value to autoreleasepool. Please see below for more about this new rule: the naming rule for methods related to object creation must be followed.

```
@autoreleasepool {
    id __strong obj = [NSMutableArray array];
}
```

Let's see the source code with comments on ownership status.

```
@autoreleasepool {
    /*
     * Obtain an object without creating it yourself and you don't have ownership
     */

    id __strong obj = [NSMutableArray array];

    /*
```

```
    * The variable obj is qualified with __strong.
    * Which means, it has ownership of the object.
    * And the object is registered in autoreleasepool,
    * because the compiler decides it by checking the method name.
    */

}
    /*
    * Leaving the scope of variable obj, its strong reference disappears.
    * The object is released automatically.
    *
    * Leaving @autoreleasepool block,
    * all the objects registered in the autoreleasepool are released automatically.
    *
    * The object is discarded because no one has ownership.
    */
```

As the example shows, objects are registered to an autoreleasepool even without the __autoreleasing qualifier. Next, let's see a sample implementation of the method, which is used in the above example to obtain an object without creating it.

```
+ (id) array
{
    return [[NSMutableArray alloc] init];
}
```

This code also doesn't use the __autoreleasing qualifier. It too can be written as follows.

```
+ (id) array
{

    id obj = [[NSMutableArray alloc] init];

    return obj;

}
```

"id obj" does not have a qualifier. So it is qualified with __strong. When the "return" sentence is executed, the variable scope is left and the strong reference disappears. Therefore the object will be released automatically. Before that, if the compiler detects that the object will be passed to the caller, the object is registered in autoreleasepool.

The next example is about the __weak ownership qualifier. As you know, the __weak ownership qualifier is used to avoid cyclic reference. When a variable with a __weak qualifier is used, the object is always registered in autoreleasepool.

```
id __weak obj1 = obj0;
NSLog(@"class=%@", [obj1 class]);
```

The above source code is equivalent to:

```
id __weak obj1 = obj0;
id __autoreleasing tmp = obj1;
NSLog(@"class=%@", [tmp class]);
```

Why does the object need to be registered in autoreleasepool in order to use the object via the __weak qualified variable? Because a variable, which is qualified with __weak, does not have a strong reference, the object might be disposed of at any point. If the object is registered in autoreleasepool, until @autoreleasepool block is left, the object must exist. So, to use the objects via __weak variable safely, the object is registered in autoreleasepool automatically.

Let's see one more final example about implicit __autoreleasing. As explained, "id obj" is the same as "id __strong obj".

How about "id *obj" ? Does it mean "id __strong *obj" ?

The answer is "id __autoreleasing *obj".

And, "NSObject **obj" means "NSObject * __autoreleasing *obj".

Any pointers to 'id' or object types are qualified with __autoreleasing as default.

Sometimes, a method passes the error information via an argument with a pointer type of NSError object instead of its return value. Cocoa Framework uses this technique for many methods such as the NSString class method stringWithContentsOfFile:encoding:error. It is like:

```
NSError *error = nil;
BOOL result = [obj performOperationWithError:&error];
```

The declaration of this method is:

```
- (BOOL) performOperationWithError:(NSError **)error;
```

Because the pointer to 'id' or object types is qualified with __autoreleasing as default, this declaration is equivalent to:

```
- (BOOL) performOperationWithError:(NSError * __autoreleasing *)error;
```

Returning a Result as the Argument

Methods taking NSError pointer as an argument need to create an NSError object itself depending on the result. The caller will obtain the object as an argument, which means that the caller does not obtain it from the alloc/new/copy/mutableCopy method group. To follow the memory management rules, when you do not obtain an object by the alloc/new/copy/mutableCopy method group, the object has to be passed without ownership. By the __autoreleasing ownership qualifier, the rule is fulfilled.

For example, performOperationWithError is implemented as follows.

```
- (BOOL) performOperationWithError:(NSError * __autoreleasing *)error
{
    /* Error occurred. Set errorCode */

    return NO;
}
```

By assigning to *error, which is NSError * __autoreleasing * type, an object can be passed to its caller after being registered in autoreleasepool.

The following source code causes a compile error.

```
NSError *error = nil;
NSError **pError = &error;
```

To assign an object pointer, both ownership qualifiers have to be the same. The compiler shows the following error.

```
error: initializing 'NSError *__autoreleasing *' with an expression
        of type 'NSError *__strong *' changes retain/release properties of pointer
        NSError **pError = &error;
                  ^          ~~~~~~
```

In this case, a __strong ownership qualifier has to be added.

```
NSError *error = nil;
NSError * __strong *pError = &error;
/* No compile error */
```

This rule applies to all the other ownership qualifiers as well.

```
NSError __weak *error = nil;
NSError * __weak *pError = &error;
/* No compile error */

NSError __unsafe_unretained *unsafeError = nil;
NSError * __unsafe_unretained *pUnsafeError = &unsafeError;
/* No compile error */
```

By the way, in the previous example, the method takes an argument as the pointer of object type, which is qualified with __autoreleasing.

```
- (BOOL) performOperationWithError:(NSError * __autoreleasing *)error;
```

And the caller passes the pointer of object type, which qualified with __strong.

```
NSError __strong *error = nil;
BOOL result = [obj performOperationWithError:&error];
```

As we have seen, to exchange object pointers, both variables must be identically qualified. But the example is not. How does it work? The following explains how the compiler handles it.

```
NSError __strong *error = nil;
NSError __autoreleasing *tmp = error;
BOOL result = [obj performOperationWithError:&tmp];
error = tmp;
```

Also, you can type the ownership qualifier explicitly for the object pointer type as follows.

```
- (BOOL) performOperationWithError:(NSError * __strong *)error;
```

This declaration shows how to pass an object without registering it to autoreleasepool. Although it is possible, you should not do that. From the caller's point of view, to create an object with ownership, the method has to be in the alloc/new/copy/mutableCopy group. If it is not in the group, the caller should obtain an object without ownership. So, the argument should be qualified with __autoreleasing.

And, when you use the __autoreleasing ownership qualifier explicitly, the variable has to be an automatic variable, such as a local variable, or an argument of method/function.

Next, let's see @autoreleasepool a bit more. In a non-ARC environment, autoreleasepools are used as follows.

```
/* non-ARC */

NSAutoreleasePool *pool0 = [[NSAutoreleasePool alloc] init];
    NSAutoreleasePool *pool1 = [[NSAutoreleasePool alloc] init];
        NSAutoreleasePool *pool2 = [[NSAutoreleasePool alloc] init];
        id obj = [[NSObject alloc] init];
        [obj autorelease];
        [pool2 drain];
    [pool1 drain];
[pool0 drain];
```

The @autoreleasepool block can be nested as well.

```
@autoreleasepool {
    @autoreleasepool {
        @autoreleasepool {
            id __autoreleasing obj = [[NSObject alloc] init];
        }
    }
}
```

For instance, Application's main function, which is generated from the iOS application template, has @autoreleasepool block to enclose all the application code.

```
int main(int argc, char *argv[])
{
    @autoreleasepool {
        return UIApplicationMain(argc, argv, nil,
            NSStringFromClass([AppDelegate class]));
    }
}
```

Also, NSRunLoop has autoreleasepool to release all the objects once in each loop. This mechanism is the same both on ARC-enabled and -disabled environments. By the way, @autoreleasepool block can be used even in a non-ARC environment, but it has to be compiled with an LLVM compiler 3.0 or later. In this case, the source code should be as follows.

```
/* non-ARC */
@autoreleasepool {
    id obj = [[NSObject alloc] init];
    [obj autorelease];
}
```

I recommend using @autoreleasepool even in a non-ARC environment, rather than NSAutoreleasePool. The reason is that the scope of autoreleasepool is written as blocks, so its readability is far better.

Also, the _objc_autoreleasePoolPrint() (see the implementation by Apple in Chapter 1) can be used for both an ARC-enabled or -disabled environment.

```
_objc_autoreleasePoolPrint();
```

Please use it effectively to debug objects in autoreleasepool.

__strong and __weak

The concept of __strong and __weak variables is very similar to that of smart pointers in C++. They are called std::shared_ptr and std::weak_ptr. std::shared_ptr uses reference counting to manage ownership of C++ class objects. Std::weak_ptr is used to avoid cyclic reference. If you have to use C++ some time, using these smart pointers is strongly recommended.

* -1999 boost::shared_ptr is part of the Boost C++ library

* 2002 boost::weak_ptr is added to the library

* 2005 tr1::shared_ptr and tr1::weak_ptr are adopted by standard C++ Library draft TR1. In some environments, std::shared_ptr and std::weak_ptr can be used

* std::shared_ptr and std::weak_ptr are adopted by C++Standard C++11 (known as C++0x)

Rules

To write and compile source code for ARC, you have to take care of a few things. Just by following the rules in the list below, you can write source code for an ARC-enabled environment with confidence.

- Forget about using retain, release, retainCount, and autorelease.

- Forget about using NSAllocateObject and NSDeallocateObject.

- Follow the naming rule for methods related to object creation.

- Forget about calling dealloc explicitly.

- Use @autoreleasepool instead of NSAutoreleasePool.

- Forget about using Zone (NSZone).

- Object type variables can't be members of struct or union in C language.

- 'id' and 'void*' have to be cast explicitly.

The rules are explained one by one.

Forget About Using Retain, Release, RetainCount, or Autorelease

As you know, the compiler will perform memory management, therefore you don't need to call memory management-related methods, such as retain, release, retainCount, and autorelease.

Apple says:

> *By enabling ARC with the new Apple LLVM compiler, you will never need to type retain or release again*

But, in reality, you can't use them. When you use them, a compile error occurs as follows.

```
error: ARC forbids explicit message send of 'release'
        [o release];
         ^ ~~~~~~~
```

So, In fact, Apple should say:

"By enabling ARC with the new Apple LLVM compiler, you can forget about the long hard days of typing retain and release."

And, the retainCount and release methods also cause compile errors, thus the following code can't be used with ARC.

```
for (;;) {
    NSUInteger count = [obj retainCount];
    [obj release];
    if (count == 1)
        break;
}
```

This source code does not fit into proper understanding of reference counting. So it should not be a problem. Anyway, retain, release, retainCount, and autorelease methods can be used only in a non-ARC environment.

Forget About Using NSAllocateObject or NSDeallocateObject

As you know, to create an object with ownership, you use an alloc method.

```
id obj = [NSObject alloc];
```

Actually, as we have seen in the implementation of alloc in GNUstep, in a non-ARC environment, it is possible to create an object and with ownership by calling

NSAllocateObject function.[2] With ARC, NSAllocateObject function can't be used. It causes a compile error as if retain were used.

```
error: 'NSAllocateObject' is unavailable:
        not available in automatic reference counting mode
```

Also, NSDeallocateObject function can't be used.

Follow the Naming Rule for Methods Related to Object Creation

As explained in Chapter 1, there are naming rules for methods related to object creation with ownership.

- alloc

- new

- copy

- mutableCopy

When an object is returned by certain methods, where the name begins with one of the above list, the caller has ownership of the object. This rule is still applicable with ARC. Also, one more prefix is added along with it.

- init

For any method where the name begins with init, there are some rules that are stricter than for the alloc/new/copy/mutableCopy method group.

The method has to be an instance method.

It has to return an object.

The return type has to be 'id' type, or types of its class, superclass, or subclass.

It returns an object without registering in autoreleasepool, as alloc/new/copy/mutableCopy method group does, which means the caller has ownership. Basically, it initializes an object, which is returned by alloc, and returns the same object as follows.

```
id obj = [[NSObject alloc] init];
```

---

[2] Apple, "Foundation Functions Reference," http://developer.apple.com/library/mac/ #documentation/Cocoa/Reference/Foundation/Miscellaneous/Foundation_Functions/ Reference/reference.html

The above source code calls the alloc method to obtain an object and then calls the init method on the same object to initialize it. After that, init method returns the same object. Now, let's see other examples.

```
- (id) initWithObject:(id)obj;
```

This method declaration meets the rules. Although the following method also meets the naming rule, it doesn't return an object, so you can't use it.

```
- (void) initThisObject;
```

Exceptionally, a method named "initialize" is not included in this init group. Therefore, you can use the following method as usual.

```
- (void) initialize;
```

Forget About Calling dealloc Explicitly

When all of the ownerships are released, the object will be discarded. It works just the same as a non-ARC environment. When disposed of, its dealloc method is called.

```
- (void) dealloc
{
    /*
     * Write here to be disposed of properly.
     */
}
```

For example, when you are using a library written in C and allocate a memory buffer, you need to free it in the dealloc method.

```
- (void) dealloc
{
    free(buffer_);
}
```

In many cases, dealloc is a suitable place to remove the object from delegate or observers.

```
- (void) dealloc
{
    [[NSNotificationCenter defaultCenter] removeObserver:self];
}
```

By the way, in a non-ARC environment, you have to type [super dealloc] every time as follows.

```
/* non-ARC */

- (void) dealloc
{
    /* Do something for this object. */

    [super dealloc];
}
```

With ARC, it causes a compile error, as when you call the release method.

```
error: ARC forbids explicit message send of 'dealloc'
        [super dealloc];
         ^      ~~~~~~~
```

You can't call [super dealloc] explicitly. It is just done automatically by ARC. You can forget typing it again and again.

Use @autoreleasepool Instead of NSAutoreleasePool

As described in the previous section, you have to use the @autoreleasepool block instead of NSAutoreleasePool. If you use the NSAutoreleasePool class, a compile error occurs.

```
error: 'NSAutoreleasePool' is unavailable:
        not available in automatic reference counting mode
        NSAutoreleasePool *pool = [[NSAutoreleasePool alloc] init];
        ^
```

Forget About Using Zone (NSZone)

With ARC, Zone (NSZone) is not usable. As explained previously (see column "Zone"), regardless of whether ARC is enabled, the recent objective-C runtime (the environment in which compiler macro __OBJC2__ is defined) just ignores zones.

Object Type Variables Cannot Be Members of struct or union in C Language

When you add a member variable of Objective-C object type to C struct or union, a compile error occurs.

```
struct Data {
    NSMutableArray *array;
};
```

```
error: ARC forbids Objective-C objs in structs or unions
    NSMutableArray *array;
                   ^
```

Even with the LLVM compiler 3.0, there is no way to manage the lifetime of C struct because of the C language spec limitation.[3] With ARC, the compiler has to know and manage an object's lifetime in order to perform memory management. For example, automatic variables (local variables) can be managed because the compiler can know

---

[3] LLVM.org "4.3.5. Ownership-qualified fields of structs and unions," http://clang.llvm.org /docs/AutomaticReferenceCounting.html#ownership.restrictions.records

the lifetime as the scope of the variable. Because there is no such information for C struct members, it is impossible for the compiler to perform memory management for C struct. If you still want to put an object to C struct, you can do it by casting the object to "void *" (see next section) or by using an __unsafe_unretained ownership qualifier (see "Ownership qualifiers" section).

```
struct Data {
      NSMutableArray __unsafe_unretained *array;
   };
```

As described previously, the compiler doesn't manage variables with the __unsafe_unretained ownership qualifier. You have to take care of ownership yourself to avoid a memory leak or the application will crash.

'id' and 'void*' Have to Be Cast Explicitly

In a non-ARC environment, casting from 'id' to 'void*' works without any problems as follows.

```
/* non-ARC */
id obj = [[NSObject alloc] init];
void *p = obj;
```

Also, it is no problem to call methods through 'id' variables, which are assigned back from void * as follows.

```
/* non-ARC */
id o = p;
[o release];
```

But these source codes cause a compile error with ARC.

```
error: implicit conversion of an Objective-C pointer
    to 'void *' is disallowed with ARC
        void *p = obj;
                  ^
```

```
    error: implicit conversion of a non-Objective-C pointer
        type 'void *' to 'id' is disallowed with ARC
        id o = p;
               ^
```

To cast between 'id' or object types and 'void*', you have to use a special kind of cast. Just for assignment, you can use __bridge cast.

__bridge cast

You can use __bridge cast as

```
id obj = [[NSObject alloc] init];

void *p = (__bridge void *)obj;

id o = (__bridge id)p;
```

With __bridge cast, you can cast 'id' to 'void*', and vice versa. But __bridge cast to void * is even more dangerous than an __unsafe_unretained qualified variable. You have to manage ownership of the object yourself carefully, or it crashes because of the dangling pointer. Also, there are two other kinds of casts: __bridge_retained and __bridge_transfer.

__bridge_retained cast

__bridge_retained cast works as if the assigned variable has ownership of the object.

```
id obj = [[NSObject alloc] init];
void *p = (__bridge_retained void *)obj;
```

The above source code can be rewritten for a non-ARC environment as follows.

```
/* non-ARC */

id obj = [[NSObject alloc] init];

void *p = obj;
[(id)p retain];
```

_bridge_retained cast has been replaced by retain. The variables "obj" and "p" have ownership of the object. Let's see other examples.

```
void *p = 0;

{
    id obj = [[NSObject alloc] init];
    p = (__bridge_retained void *)obj;
}

NSLog(@"class=%@", [(__bridge id)p class]);
```

When leaving the scope of variable obj, its strong reference disappears and the object is released. Because variable p also has ownership, the object is not discarded. Let's rewrite it for a non-ARC environment as usual.

```
/* non-ARC */

void *p = 0;

{
    id obj = [[NSObject alloc] init];
    /* [obj retainCount] -> 1 */

    p = [obj retain];
    /* [obj retainCount] -> 2 */

    [obj release];
    /* [obj retainCount] -> 1 */}


    /*
     * [(id)p retainCount] -> 1
     * which means,
```

```
 * [obj retainCount] -> 1
 * So, the object still exists.
 */
```

```
NSLog(@"class=%@", [(__bridge id)p class]);
```

Conversely, __bridge_transfer cast will release the object just after the assignment is done.

__bridge_transfer cast

You can use __bridge_transfer cast as

```
id obj = (__bridge_transfer id)p;
```

This source code can be rewritten for a non-ARC environment.

```
/* non-ARC */
id obj = (id)p;
[obj retain];
[(id)p release];
```

As __bridge_retained cast is replaced with retain, __bridge_transfer cast is replaced with release. The variable obj is retained because it is qualified with __strong. With these two casts, you can create, own, and release any objects without using 'id' or object type variables. But it is not recommended. Please be careful when you use them. Let's see one more example.

```
void *p = (__bridge_retained void *)[[NSObject alloc] init];
NSLog(@"class=%@", [(__bridge id)p class]);
(void)(__bridge_transfer id)p;
```

This source code can be rewritten for a non-ARC environment as follows.

```
/* non-ARC */

id p = [[NSObject alloc] init];
NSLog(@"class=%@", [p class]);
[p release];
```

These casts are used frequently to convert Objective-C objects and Core Foundation objects.

OBJECTIVE-C OBJECT AND CORE FOUNDATION OBJECT

A Core Foundation object is an object used with the Core Foundation Framework. It is mainly written in C and has a reference count. In the Core Foundation framework, CFRetain and CFRelease are the equivalent functions to retain and release in Objective-C in a non-ARC environment.

The difference between a Core Foundation object and an Objective-C object is very small. It is more or less how it is created, either with Foundation framework (Cocoa) in Objective-C or with Core Foundation framework. After being created, it can be used transparently in both frameworks' manner. For instance, even when an object is created with the Foundation Framework API, it can be released with the Core Foundation Framework API or vice versa.

Actually there is no difference between a Core Foundation object itself and an Objective-C object itself. So, to cast the object, in a non-ARC environment, just using a C language style cast is enough. This conversion is called a Toll-Free Bridge because just casting has no cost for the CPU.

You can see the list of Toll-Free Bridge classes in the following document.

Toll-Free Bridged Types
http://developer.apple.com/library/mac/documentation/CoreFoundation/Conceptual/
CFDesignConcepts/Articles/tollFreeBridgedTypes.html

For an ARC-enabled environment, to convert an object between Objective-C and Core Foundation, in other words, for a Toll-Free Bridge cast, the following functions are provided.

```
CFTypeRef CFBridgingRetain(id X) {
    return (__bridge_retained CFTypeRef)X;
}

id CFBridgingRelease(CFTypeRef X) {
    return (__bridge_transfer id)X;
}
```

Let's see how we can use these functions.

CFBridgingRetain function

Listing 2–11 creates an NSMutableArray object with ownership and uses the object as a Core Foundation object.

Listing 2–11. *CFBridgingRetain*

```
CFMutableArrayRef cfObject = NULL;
{
    id obj = [[NSMutableArray alloc] init];
    cfObject = CFBridgingRetain(obj);
    CFShow(cfObject);
    printf("retain count = %d\n", CFGetRetainCount(cfObject));
}
printf("retain count after the scope = %d\n", CFGetRetainCount(cfObject));
CFRelease(cfObject);
```

The result is as follows. () means an empty array.

```
()
retain count = 2
retain count after the scope = 1
```

Now we've learned that an Objective-C object in the Foundation Framework can be used as a Core Foundation object. Also the object can be released with CFRelease. In the example, you can also use __bridge_retained cast instead of CFBridgingRetain as follows. Just choose whichever you like.

```
CFMutableArrayRef cfObject = (__bridge_retained CFMutableArrayRef)obj;
```

Let's see the source code with comments on ownership status and the value of CFGetRetainCount (Listing 2–12).

Listing 2–12. *CFBridgingRetain with comments*

```
CFMutableArrayRef cfObject = NULL;
{
    id obj = [[NSMutableArray alloc] init];

     /*
      * variable obj has a strong reference to the object
      */
    cfObject = CFBridgingRetain(obj);

     /*
      * CFBridgingRetain works as if CFRetain is called and
      * the object is assigned to variable cfObject
      */

    CFShow(cfObject);
    printf("retain count = %d\n", CFGetRetainCount(cfObject));

     /*
      * Reference count is two.  One is for strong reference of variable obj,
      * The other is by CFBridgingRetain.
      */
}

 /*
  * Leaving the scope of variable obj, its strong reference disappears.
  * Reference count is one.
  */

printf("retain count after the scope = %d\n", CFGetRetainCount(cfObject));
CFRelease(cfObject);

/*
* Reference count is zero because of CFRelease.
* So, the object is discarded.
*/
```

Next, let's see what will happen if __bridge cast is used instead of CFBridgingRetain or __bridge_retained cast (Listing 2–13).

Listing 2–13. *__bridge cast is used instead of __bridge_retained cast*

```
CFMutableArrayRef cfObject = NULL;
{
    id obj = [[NSMutableArray alloc] init];

     /*
      * variable obj has a strong reference to the object
      */

    cfObject = (__bridge CFMutableArrayRef)obj;
    CFShow(cfObject);
    printf("retain count = %d\n", CFGetRetainCount(cfObject));

     /*
      * __bridge cast does not touch ownership status.
      * Reference count is one because of variable obj's strong reference.
```

```
        */
}

/*
 * Leaving the scope of variable obj, its strong reference disappears.
 * The object is released automatically.
 * Because no one has ownership, the object is discarded.
 */

/*
 * From here, any access to the object is invalid! (dangling pointer)
 */

printf("retain count after the scope = %d\n", CFGetRetainCount(cfObject));
CFRelease(cfObject);
```

Now, we understand why CFBridgingRetain or __bridge_retained cast is needed.

CFBridgingRelease function

Listing 2–14 shows how to create an NSMutableArray object with a Core Foundation API in an opposite manner. It uses the CFBridgingRelease function.

Listing 2–14. *Creating NSMutableArray object*

```
{
    CFMutableArrayRef cfObject =
        CFArrayCreateMutable(kCFAllocatorDefault, 0, NULL);
    printf("retain count = %d\n", CFGetRetainCount(cfObject));
    id obj = CFBridgingRelease(cfObject);
    printf("retain count after the cast = %d\n", CFGetRetainCount(cfObject));
    NSLog(@"class=%@", obj);
}
```

You can see that the object is created with ownership by the Core Foundation Framework API. As the opposite of the previous example, the object is used as an Objective-C object, The result is as follows.

```
retain count = 1
retain count after the cast = 1
```

Of course you can use bridge_transfer instead of CFBridgingRelease.

```
id obj = (__bridge_transfer id)cfObject;
```

And, let's see the source code with comments on ownership status as usual (Listing 2–15).

Listing 2–15. *Creating NSMutableArray object with comments*

```
{
    CFMutableArrayRef cfObject =
    CFArrayCreateMutable(kCFAllocatorDefault, 0, NULL);
    printf("retain count = %d\n", CFGetRetainCount(cfObject));

    /*
     * The object is created with ownership by Core Foundation Framework API.
     * The retain count is one.
     */
```

```
        id obj = CFBridgingRelease(cfObject);

        /*
         * By assignment  after CFBridgingRelease,
         * variable obj has a strong reference and then
         * the object is released by CFRelease.
         */

        printf("retain count after the cast = %d\n", CFGetRetainCount(cfObject));

        /*
         * Only the variable obj has a strong reference to
         * the object, so the retain count is one.
         *
         * And, after being cast by CFBridgingRelease,
         * pointer stored in variable cfObject is still valid.
         */

        NSLog(@"class=%@", obj);
}

    /*
     * Leaving the scope of variable obj, its strong reference disappears.
     * The object is released automatically.
     * Because no one has ownership, the object is discarded.
     */
```

Let's see what happens when __bridge cast is used instead of CFBridgingRelease or __bridge_transfer cast (Listing 2–16).

Listing 2–16. *__bridge cast is used instead of __bridge_transfer cast*

```
{
    CFMutableArrayRef cfObject =
    CFArrayCreateMutable(kCFAllocatorDefault, 0, NULL);
    printf("retain count = %d\n", CFGetRetainCount(cfObject));

        /*
         * The object is created with ownership by Core Foundation Framework API.
         * The retain count is one.
         */

    id obj = (__bridge id)cfObject;

        /*
         * variable obj has a strong reference because it is qualified with __strong.
         */

    printf("retain count after the cast = %d\n", CFGetRetainCount(cfObject));

        /*
         * Because variable obj has a strong reference and
         * CFRelease is not called,
         * retain count is two.
         */

    NSLog(@"class=%@", obj);
```

```
}
/*
 * Leaving the scope of variable obj, its strong reference disappears.
 * The object is released.
 */

/*
 * Because the reference count is one, it is not discarded. Memory leak!
 */
```

As shown in the above example, you have to use CFBridgingRetain/CFBridgingRelease or __bridge_retained/__bridge_transfer cast properly. When you need to assign Objective-C objects to variables of C type, such as void*, you have to implement it with the utmost care.

Property

With ARC, new modifiers are introduced for the Objective-C class property as follows.

```
@property (nonatomic, strong) NSString *name;
```

As a property modifier, you can use the qualifiers listed in Table 2–1 in an ARC-enabled environment.

Table 2–1. *Property modifier and ownership qualifier table*

Property modifier	Ownership qualifier
assign	__unsafe_unretained
copy	__strong (note: new copied object is assigned.)
retain	__strong
strong	__strong
unsafe_unretained	__unsafe_unretained
weak	__weak

Assigning to a property is the same as assigning to a variable with a corresponding ownership qualifier. A copy modifier is not just an assignment. It copies the object by using NSCopying protocol copyWithZone: method and then assigning it.

When you manually declare an instance variable for the property as well, it has to have the same ownership qualifier as the property. Let's see it with an example.

```
i
@interface SomeObject : NSObject {
    id obj;
}
@end
```

The member variable obj is declared as an 'id' type. At the same time, if the property is declared with a weak ownership qualifier as:

```
@property (nonatomic, weak) id obj;
```

it causes a compile error.

```
error: existing ivar 'obj' for __weak property 'obj' must be __weak
    @synthesize obj;
              ^
    note: property declared here
    @property (nonatomic, weak) id obj;
                                  ^
```

In this case, the member variable must be qualified with __weak.

```
@interface SomeObject : NSObject {
    id _weak obj;
} @end
```

Or, the property has to have the modifier "strong".

```
@property (nonatomic, strong) id obj;
```

Next, let's see what you should know when using an array with ARC.

Array

I explained the ownership specifiers with 'id' or object type variables. In this section, I explain how we can use the specifiers with arrays.

The following source code shows how to use a static array of variables qualified with __strong.

```
id objs[10];
```

You can do the same with __weak, __autoreleasing, or __unsafe_unretained.

```
id __weak objs[10];
```

By the way, any variables qualified with __strong, __weak, or __autoreleasing other than __unsafe_unretained, are initialized with nil. This is also applied for static array. Any arrays of variables, which qualified with __strong, __weak, or __autoreleasing, are initialized with nil. Let's see how to use them.

```
{
    id objs[2];
    objs[0] = [[NSObject alloc] init];
    objs[1] = [NSMutableArray array];
}
```

When the control flow leaves the scope of the array, all the variables that have strong references in the array disappear. The assigned objects are released automatically. It is identical to variables not in arrays.

What will happen with a dynamic array? Basically, you should use containers in the Foundation Framework such as NSMutableArray, NSMutableDictionary, or

NSMutableSet. Then the stored objects will be properly managed. These containers are the better choice, but you can still use a dynamic C array with variables qualified with __strong. But you have to remember a few things. As usual, let's see them with an example.

First, declare a pointer to a dynamic C array:

```
id __strong *array = nil;
```

As described previously, 'id *' type means 'id __autoreleasing *'. So, in this case, you have to type __strong qualifier. Although 'id' type variables with a __strong ownership qualifier are initialized as nil, id pointer type variables qualified with __strong are not. So, you have to assign nil explicitly.

Or, you can declare it as follows, if you prefer class type instead of 'id'.

```
NSObject * __strong *array = nil;
```

Next, allocate a memory block for the variables in the array with the calloc function.

```
array = (id __strong *)calloc(entries, sizeof(id));
```

In this source code, a memory block is allocated for the number of "entries" elements. Note that variables qualified with __strong have to be initialized with nil. The calloc function is used to fill with zero after allocation. Instead of the calloc function, you can use the malloc function to allocate and the memset function to fill with zero as follows.

```
array = (id __strong *)malloc(entries * sizeof(id));
memset(array, 0, entries * sizeof(id));
```

However, it is very dangerous to assign nil as follows.

```
array = (id __strong *)malloc(sizeof(id) * entries);
for (NSUInteger i = 0; i < entries; ++i)
    array[i] = nil;
```

In this source code, the memory area allocated by malloc isn't initialized by zero. So, before each assignment, release methods are called on invalid addresses. Therefore simply using the calloc function is recommended. After that, you can do anything for the dynamic array that you can for the static array.

```
array[0] = [[NSObject alloc] init];
```

But after you finish using a dynamic array of variables qualified with __strong, you have to release all the entries yourself. This is very different from static array. Just disposing of the memory block with free function as in the following causes a memory leak because each entry will never be released.

```
free(array);
```

For static arrays, the compiler will insert code to release all the entries automatically when the variable scope is left. But for dynamic arrays, the compiler can't detect their lifetimes. By setting all the entries to nil, you can remove all the strong references of the entries so that all the objects will be released. And then, you have to dispose of the memory block itself as well.

```
for (NSUInteger i = 0; i < entries; ++i)
    array[i] = nil;
```

```
free(array);
```

As opposed to the initialization, you can't release objects with the memset function as it causes memory leak. It is just dangerous. You have to assign nil to all the entries manually to let the compiler detect it.

Likewise, copying any entries by memcpy or realloc the memory block is dangerous as well. By doing so the object might not be disposed of, or the same object might be disposed of more than once. So, using these functions is strictly prohibited.

Also, you can use dynamic arrays of variables qualified with __weak in the same manner as with __strong. It is better not to use with __autoreleasing, because that produces an unexpected state. Because any variables qualified with __unsafe_unretained are not in control of the compiler, you can use them just as you would C pointer type variables such as void*.

Summary

In this chapter, we learned:

- How the reference counting rules are still applicable with ARC

- The ownership qualifiers that are newly added with ARC

- New properties that are added for ARC

- Rules you must know to use ARC

In the next chapter, we discuss these items in detail with the implementation of ARC itself.

Chapter **3**

ARC Implementation

In this chapter, we discuss the implementation of ARC itself to review what we learned in the last chapter, explaining in detail what ARC is and how it works.

Apple says, "Automatic Reference Counting (ARC) in Objective-C makes memory management the job of the compiler," but the truth is, ARC isn't the only job of the compiler. The objective-C runtime needs to help as well, so ARC is actually achieved by both tool and library:

- Compiler: clang (LLVM compiler) 3.0 or later

- Objective-C runtime library: objc4 493.9 or later

NOTE: As Apple says, if ARC is the only compiler's job, the __weak ownership specifier can also be usable on iOS4 or OS X Snow Leopard.

When the application is compiled for iOS4 or OS X Snow Leopard, libarclite_iphoneos.a or libarclite_macosx.a is linked to make ARC work. Even if the ARC supporting library is linked, it is still impossible to set nil for the __weak qualified variable after the object is discarded (zeroing weak references). I guess that it is a limitation of legacy frameworks and the runtime library. Inasmuch as we can't see the source code of libarclite, it is just my guess, though.

For now, however, let's not worry about the older operating systems; instead in this chapter we concentrate on the implementations of ARC itself and look at the output of clang assembler and the source codes of runtime/objc-arr.mm in the objc4 library.

In the following sections, we show ARC's source code for each qualifier. We've already learned what the qualifiers are and how we use them. In the following sections we learn how they work in detail. Let's start with the __strong ownership qualifier.

__strong ownership qualifier

Let's see how the variables that are qualified with __strong work, using NSMutableArray class method "array" as an example. We see under the hood of calling the method and inside the method itself. Before that, please see the following source code.

```
{
    id __strong obj = [[NSObject alloc] init];
}
```

Clang can display its output as assembly/machine code. For the sake of readability we have represented each excerpt below as its ObjC equivalent. With the output and the source code of the objc4 library, we are able to see what is going on under the hood. The above source code is rewritten as follows. Please note that sometimes we use pseudo code to make it more understandable.

```
/* pseudo code by the compiler */
id obj = objc_msgSend(NSObject, @selector(alloc));
objc_msgSend(obj, @selector(init));
objc_release(obj);
```

You can see that objc_msgSend is called twice for alloc and init method invocation. After that, objc_release is called to release the object when the variable scope is left. Although you can't call the release method explicitly, you can see that release is automatically inserted in the pseudo code.

Calling the array method

Next, let's see what happens when an object is not obtained by the alloc/new/copy/mutableCopy method group. The original source code is as follows.

```
{
    id __strong obj = [NSMutableArray array];
}
```

This is ordinary-looking NSMutableArray class method "array". The pseudo code of this is a bit different from the previous one.

```
/* pseudo code by the compiler */
id obj = objc_msgSend(NSMutableArray, @selector(array));
objc_retainAutoreleasedReturnValue(obj);
objc_release(obj);
```

The first objc_msgSend for the array method and the last objc_release are the same as the previous one. What is the objc_retainAutoreleasedReturnValue function call?

objc_retainAutoreleasedReturnValue function is for performance optimization. It is inserted because the NSMutableArray class method array is not in the alloc/new/copy/mutableCopy method group. The compiler inserts this function every time just after the invocation of a method if the method is not in the group. As the name suggests, it retains an object returned from a method or function after the object is added in autorelease pool.

objc_retainAutoreleasedReturnValue function expects that an objc_autoreleaseReturnValue function has been called inside the method. Any methods, that are not in the alloc/new/copy/mutableCopy group, have to call objc_autoreleaseReturnValue. For instance, NSMutableArray class method "array" calls this function.

Inside the array Method

Let's see the implementation of the NSMutableArray class method "array" as the compiler-generated code.

```
+ (id) array
{
    return [[NSMutableArray alloc] init];
}
```

This source code is converted as follows. It calls objc_autoreleaseReturnValue function at the last.

```
/* pseudo code by the compiler */
+ (id) array
{
    id obj = objc_msgSend(NSMutableArray, @selector(alloc));
    objc_msgSend(obj, @selector(init));
    return objc_autoreleaseReturnValue(obj);
}
```

Any methods that return an object added to autorelease pool call objc_autoreleaseReturnValue function as in the above example. It adds an object to autorelease pool and returns it. But, in reality, objc_autoreleaseReturnValue doesn't register it to autorelease pool all the time.

objc_autoreleaseReturnValue checks the caller's executable code and if the code calls objc_retainAutoreleasedReturnValue function just after calling this method, it skips registering to the autorelease pool and just returns the object to the caller. objc_retainAutoreleasedReturnValue function is implemented to obtain such an object properly even if objc_autoreleaseReturnValue didn't register the object to the autorelease pool. By co-operation of objc_autoreleaseReturnValue and objc_retainAutoreleasedReturnValue, the object bypasses being added to autorelease pool as shown in Figure3–1. So, performance will be improved.[1]

---

[1] With objc4 version 493.9, the optimization works only in an OS X 64-bit environment.

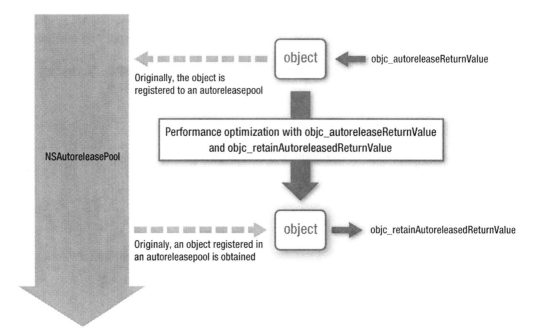

Figure 3–1. *Skip registration to the autorelease pool*

__weak ownership qualifier

Next, we learn about the __weak ownership qualifier. We show what happens when an object is disposed of or when a newly created object is assigned and how an object is added to the autorelease pool automatically.

As described previously in Chapter 2, the __weak ownership qualifier provides the following features.

- Nil is assigned to any variables qualified with __weak when referencing object is discarded.

- When an object is accessed through a __weak qualified variable, the object is added to the autorelease pool.

Let's start with the following example to see what is going on behind the scenes.

```
{
    id __weak obj1 = obj;
}
```

Here, assume that the variable obj is stored in some variables qualified with __strong.

```
/* pseudo code by the compiler */
id obj1;
objc_initWeak(&obj1, obj);
objc_destroyWeak(&obj1);
```

The variable qualified with __weak is initialized by the objc_initWeak function. When the variable scope is left, the objc_destroyWeak function destroys it.

The objc_initWeak function is implemented as the following source code. It clears the variable qualified with __weak, and then calls the objc_storeWeak function with the object to be assigned.

```
obj1 = 0;
objc_storeWeak(&obj1, obj);
```

The objc_destroyWeak function calls objc_storeWeak function with zero as argument as follows.

```
objc_storeWeak(&obj1, 0);
```

So, the example code is equivalent to:

```
/* pseudo code by the compiler */
id obj1;
obj1 = 0;
objc_storeWeak(&obj1, obj);
objc_storeWeak(&obj1, 0);
```

objc_storeWeak function registers a key-value to a table, called a weak table. The key is the second argument, the address of the object to be assigned. The value is the first argument, the address of a variable that qualified with __weak. If the second argument is zero, the entry is removed from the table.

The weak table is implemented as a hash table as a reference count table (see Chapter 1, Section "The Implementation by Apple"). With that, variables qualified with __weak can be searched from a disposing object with reasonable performance. When the function is called with the same object for key, multiple __weak qualified variables will be registered for the same object.

Looking Under the Hood When an Object Is Discarded

Next, let's see the function calls when an object is disposed of when no one has ownership of it. Objects are relinquished by objc_release function.

1. objc_release.

2. dealloc is called because retain count becomes zero.

3. _objc_rootDealloc.

4. object_dispose.

5. objc_destructInstance.

6. objc_clear_deallocating.

objc_clear_deallocating function is called last. It does the following.

1. From the weak table, get an entry of which the key is the object to be discarded.

2. Set nil to all the __weak ownership qualified variables in the entry.

3. Remove the entry from the table.

4. For the object to be disposed of, remove its key from the reference table.

This is the implementation and it lets us know how nil is assigned to any variables qualified with __weak when the referencing object is discarded. Also, it tells us that if too many __weak ownership qualified variables are used, it consumes CPU resources at some level. So, __weak ownership qualified variables should be used only to avoid circular references.

Assigning a Newly Created Object

As described previously, the following source code causes a warning.

```
{
    id __weak obj = [[NSObject alloc] init];
}
```

It tries to assign a new object to a variable. But no one can have ownership because the variable is qualified with __weak. So, the object is immediately released and discarded. That is the reason for the warning.

```
warning: assigning retained obj to weak variable; obj will be
        released after assignment [-Warc-unsafe-retained-assign]
            id __weak obj = [[NSObject alloc] init];
                ^         ~~~~~~~~~~~~~~~~~
```

Let's see how the compiler handles the source code.

```
/* pseudo code by the compiler */
id obj;
id tmp = objc_msgSend(NSObject, @selector(alloc));
objc_msgSend(tmp, @selector(init));
objc_initWeak(&obj, tmp);
objc_release(tmp);
objc_destroyWeak(&object);
```

objc_initWeak function assigns the new object to the variable, which is qualified with __weak. Also, the compiler detects that no one has ownership and inserts the objc_release function.

When objc_release is called, the object will be discarded and the variable qualified with __weak becomes nil. Let's check the result with NSLog:

```
{
```

```
    id __weak obj = [[NSObject alloc] init];
    NSLog(@"obj=%@", obj);
}
```

The result is as follows. It shows nil formatted with "%@".

```
obj=(null)
```

What will happen if an object is created and just discarded? Let's see it in the next section with its implementation.

Immediate Disposal of Objects

As we described, the following source code causes a compiler warning.

```
id __weak obj = [[NSObject alloc] init];
```

This is because the compiler detects that no one has ownership of the new object. How about __unsafe_unretained?

```
id __unsafe_unretained obj = [[NSObject alloc] init];
```

The same as __weak, the compiler detects that no one has ownership of the object.

```
warning: assigning retained object to unsafe_unretained variable;
        obj will be released after assignment [-Warc-unsafe-retained-assign]
        id __unsafe_unretained obj = [[NSObject alloc] init];
                                   ^   ~~~~~~~~~~~~~~~~
```

The source code is equivalent to:

```
/* pseudo code by the compiler */
id obj = objc_msgSend(NSObject, @selector(alloc));
objc_msgSend(obj, @selector(init));
objc_release(obj);
```

The new object is released by the objc_release function, and the variable obj still has a dangling pointer. What will happen if the object is not assigned to any variables? Without ARC, it just causes a memory leak.

```
[[NSObject alloc] init];
```

With ARC, the compiler gives a warning because the returned value is never used.

```
warning: expression result unused [-Wunused-value]
    [[NSObject alloc] init];
    ^~~~~~~~~~~~~~~
```

You can hide the warning by casting it to void.

```
(void)[[NSObject alloc] init];
```

This source code is converted to the following, with or without cast.

```
/* pseudo code by the compiler */
id tmp = objc_msgSend(NSObject, @selector(alloc));
objc_msgSend(tmp, @selector(init));
objc_release(tmp);
```

Unless the object is not assigned to a variable, the code is the same as with __unsafe_unretained. Because no one has ownership, the compiler generates an objc_release function call. Because of ARC, no memory leak occurs.

One more question: can we call instance methods for these immediately disposed of objects as follows?

```
(void)[[[NSObject alloc] init] hash];
```

This is equivalent to:

```
/* pseudo code by the compiler */
id tmp = objc_msgSend(NSObject, @selector(alloc));
objc_msgSend(tmp, @selector(init));
objc_msgSend(tmp, @selector(hash));
objc_release(tmp);
```

The object is released after the method is called. The compiler handles memory management properly as Apple says!

Adding to autorelease pool Automatically

As described previously, when an object is accessed through a __weak qualified variable, the object has been added to the autorelease pool. Let's see how it works.

```
{
    id __weak obj1 = obj;
    NSLog(@"%@", obj1);
}
```

The source code is equivalent to the following.

```
/* pseudo code by the compiler */
id obj1;
objc_initWeak(&obj1, obj);
id tmp = objc_loadWeakRetained(&obj1);
objc_autorelease(tmp);
NSLog(@"%@", tmp);
objc_destroyWeak(&obj1);
```

objc_loadWeakRetained and objc_autorelease function calls are newly inserted, which are not in the previous examples. This is because the variable is used somehow. These functions do the following.

1.　objc_loadWeakRetained function retains the object referenced by the variable qualified with __weak.

2.　objc_autorelease function adds the object to the autorelease pool.

This means that an object assigned to a variable with __weak, is added to the autorelease pool so that the variable can be used safely until @autoreleasepool block is left.

> **NOTE:** If you use __weak qualified variables too often, too many objects will be stored in autorelease pool.

To avoid this storage issue, I recommend that when you use a __weak qualified variable, you should assign the object to a __strong qualified variable as well. For example, the next example uses variable o five times, which is qualified with __weak.

```
{
    id __weak o = obj;
    NSLog(@"1 %@", o);
    NSLog(@"2 %@", o);
    NSLog(@"3 %@", o);
    NSLog(@"4 %@", o);
    NSLog(@"5 %@", o);
}
```

The object is added to the autorelease pool five times:

```
objc[14481]: ##############
objc[14481]: AUTORELEASE POOLS for thread 0xad0892c0
objc[14481]: 6 releases pending.
objc[14481]: [0x6a85000]  ...............  PAGE  (hot) (cold)
objc[14481]: [0x6a85028]  ###############  POOL 0x6a85028
objc[14481]: [0x6a8502c]          0x6719e40  NSObject
objc[14481]: [0x6a85030]          0x6719e40  NSObject
objc[14481]: [0x6a85034]          0x6719e40  NSObject
objc[14481]: [0x6a85038]          0x6719e40  NSObject
objc[14481]: [0x6a8503c]          0x6719e40  NSObject
objc[14481]: ##############
```

You can avoid that by assigning the object to a variable qualified with __strong.

```
{
    id __weak o = obj;
    id tmp = o;
    NSLog(@"1 %@", tmp);
    NSLog(@"2 %@", tmp);
    NSLog(@"3 %@", tmp);
    NSLog(@"4 %@", tmp);
    NSLog(@"5 %@", tmp);
}
```

In this case, the object is added to the autorelease pool just once at the line "tmp = o;"

```
objc[14481]: ##############
objc[14481]: AUTORELEASE POOLS for thread 0xad0892c0
objc[14481]: 2 releases pending.
objc[14481]: [0x6a85000]  ...............  PAGE  (hot) (cold)
objc[14481]: [0x6a85028]  ###############  POOL 0x6a85028
objc[14481]: [0x6a8502c]          0x6719e40  NSObject
objc[14481]: ##############
```

As described previously, a __weak qualifier can't be used for iOS4 or OS X Snow Leopard. Also, in some other cases, a __weak ownership qualifier can't be used because some classes don't support __weak qualified variables.

For example, an NSMachPort class can't be assigned to any variables qualified with __weak. These classes override retain/release and have their own reference counts in their original implementation. When an object is assigned to a __weak qualified variable, the compiler has to insert objc4 functions properly, so many of these classes can't support a __weak qualification. These unsupported classes have an attribute __attribute__((objc_arc_weak_reference_unavailable)) in class declaration, which is defined as NS_AUTOMATED_REFCOUNT_WEAK_UNAVAILABLE. Even if you assign an object of these classes to a variable, qualified with __weak, the compiler properly generates an error. These classes are very rare, so you don't need to worry about it too much.

ALLOWSWEAKREFERENCE AND RETAINWEAKREFERENCE METHODS

There is the other case where you can't use the __weak ownership qualifier. When an NSObject instance method allowsWeakReference or retainWeakReference returns NO, the object can't be assigned to a variable qualified with __weak. These methods are not documented in the NSObject protocol. The declaration is as follows.

```
- (BOOL)allowsWeakReference;
- (BOOL)retainWeakReference;
```

When an object is assigned to a variable qualified with __weak, allowsWeakReference is called. If it returns NO, your application will be aborted:

```
cannot form weak reference to instance (0x753e180) of class MyObject
```

This means you should not assign an object of such a class to a variable qualified with __weak. You should be able to know if the class has such a restriction in the class reference.

When retainWeakReference method returns NO, the user gets value nil. Let's see it with an example.

```
{
    id __strong obj = [[NSObject alloc] init];
    id __weak o = obj;
    NSLog(@"1 %@", o);
    NSLog(@"2 %@", o);
    NSLog(@"3 %@", o);
    NSLog(@"4 %@", o);
    NSLog(@"5 %@", o);
}
```

The object exists until the scope of the variable obj is left. Therefore the variable o is usable during that time. The result is as follows.

```
1 <NSObject: 0x753e180>
2 <NSObject: 0x753e180>
3 <NSObject: 0x753e180>
4 <NSObject: 0x753e180>
5 <NSObject: 0x753e180>
```

Let's see what happens if retainWeakReference returns NO. The next source code illustrates how retainWeakReference can be implemented.

```
@interface MyObject : NSObject
{
    NSUInteger count;
```

```
}
@end

@implementation MyObject
- (id)init
{
    self = [super init];
    return self;
}
- (BOOL)retainWeakReference
{
    if (++count > 3)
        return NO;
    return [super retainWeakReference];
}
@end
```

In this example, retainWeakReference method returns NO when it is called more than three times. And the above example is modified from NSObject to MyObject.

```
{
    id __strong obj = [[MyObject alloc] init];
    id __weak o = obj;
    NSLog(@"1 %@", o);
    NSLog(@"2 %@", o);
    NSLog(@"3 %@", o);
    NSLog(@"4 %@", o);
    NSLog(@"5 %@", o);
}
```

The result is as follows.

```
1 <MyObject: 0x753e180>
2 <MyObject: 0x753e180>
3 <MyObject: 0x753e180>
4 (null)
5 (null)
```

When retainWeakReference method returns NO, the object can't be accessed. If some classes in Framework use this mechanism, the class reference should have a comment about that. Also, allowsWeakReference and retainWeakReference methods are called by the runtime library in the middle of __weak qualification-related procedures. So, if some runtime library APIs are called inside these methods, your application might hang. These methods are undocumented and an application developer shouldn't implement them. But if you need to implement them for any reason, you need to have a good understanding of how they work.

__autoreleasing ownership qualifier

Assigning an object to any variables qualified with __autoreleasing is equivalent to calling the autorelease method in a non-ARC environment. Let's see how it works with source code.

```
@autoreleasepool {
    id __autoreleasing obj = [[NSObject alloc] init];
}
```

It adds an object of NSObject class to the autorelease pool. Let's see how the compiler translates it.

```
/* pseudo code by the compiler */
id pool = objc_autoreleasePoolPush();
id obj = objc_msgSend(NSObject, @selector(alloc));
objc_msgSend(obj, @selector(init));
objc_autorelease(obj);
objc_autoreleasePoolPop(pool);
```

It just works as I explained with Apple's implementation. (See Chapter 1, Section "Apple's Implementation of autorelease.") The autorelease mechanism itself works exactly same as in a non-ARC environment although the source codes are different.

What happens if the object is not obtained by the alloc/new/copy/mutableCopy method group? Let's see the next example with NSMutableArray class method "array".

```
@autoreleasepool {
    id __autoreleasing obj = [NSMutableArray array];
}
```

Let's check what is different from the previous example.

```
/* pseudo code by the compiler */
id pool = objc_autoreleasePoolPush();
id obj = objc_msgSend(NSMutableArray, @selector(array));
objc_retainAutoreleasedReturnValue(obj);
objc_autorelease(obj);
objc_autoreleasePoolPop(pool);
```

Although, objc_retainAutoreleasedReturnValue is used, other autorelease pool-related codes are exactly the same as the previous example.

__unsafe_unretained ownership qualifier

The last ownership qualifier is __unsafe_unretained. As I explained in the Section "Immediate Disposal of Objects," assignment to a variable that is qualified with __unsafe_unretained never appears in pseudo code. Unlike the other ownership qualifiers, the compiler does nothing special for the qualifier. It just works as an assignment in C language.

Now we learned the implementations of each ownership qualifier. You should now have a better understanding of ARC. In the last chapters, the number of reference counts is not discussed much. In the next section, I explain it at last.

Reference Count

In this book, the number of reference counts itself is intentionally not explained much because to have the correct perspective on reference counting, you should not care for the number itself. If you still want to know the actual number, you can find it with:

```
uintptr_t _objc_rootRetainCount(id obj)
```

By calling the _objc_rootRetainCount function, you can get the reference count number. Let's see an example.

```
{
    id __strong obj = [[NSObject alloc] init];
    NSLog(@"retain count = %d", _objc_rootRetainCount(obj));
}
```

In the source code, the variable obj only has a strong reference. So, it displays:

```
retain count = 1
```

Let's check it with the__weak ownership qualifier as well.

```
{
    id __strong obj = [[NSObject alloc] init];
    id __weak o = obj;
    NSLog(@"retain count = %d", _objc_rootRetainCount(obj));
}
```

A variable qualified with __weak does not have ownership, so the value should not be changed.

```
retain count = 1
```

Yes, it is just as we expected. How about this with __autoreleasing?

```
@autoreleasepool {
    id __strong obj = [[NSObject alloc] init];
    id __autoreleasing o = obj;
    NSLog(@"retain count = %d", _objc_rootRetainCount(obj));
}
```

The result is:

```
retain count = 2
```

It is two due to a strong reference and having been added to an autorelease pool. Let's see the value after leaving @autoreleasepool block.

```
{
    id __strong obj = [[NSObject alloc] init];
    @autoreleasepool {
        id __autoreleasing o = obj;
        NSLog(@"retain count = %d in @autoreleasepool", _objc_rootRetainCount(obj));
    }
    NSLog(@"retain count = %d", _objc_rootRetainCount(obj));
}
```

Here is the result.

```
retain count = 2 in @autoreleasepool
retain count = 1
```

The object is released as expected.

Also, let's confirm that an object will be added to an autorelease pool, when the object is used through a variable qualified with __weak. We can see the status of autorelease pool by objc_autoreleasePoolPrint function.

```
@autoreleasepool {
    id __strong obj = [[NSObject alloc] init];
    _objc_autoreleasePoolPrint();
    id __weak o = obj;
    NSLog(@"before using __weak: retain count = %d", _objc_rootRetainCount(obj));
    NSLog(@"class = %@", [o class]);
    NSLog(@"after using __weak: retain count = %d", _objc_rootRetainCount(obj));
    _objc_autoreleasePoolPrint();
}
```

The result is:

```
objc[14481]: ##############
objc[14481]: AUTORELEASE POOLS for thread 0xad0892c0
objc[14481]: 1 releases pending.
objc[14481]: [0x6a85000]  ...............  APAGE  (hot) (cold)
objc[14481]: [0x6a85028]  ###############  POOL 0x6a85028
objc[14481]: ##############
before using __weak: retain count = 1
class = NSObject
after using __weak: retain count = 2
objc[14481]: ##############
objc[14481]: AUTORELEASE POOLS for thread 0xad0892c0
objc[14481]: 2 releases pending.
objc[14481]: [0x6a85000]  ...............  PAGE  (hot) (cold)
objc[14481]: [0x6a85028]  ###############  POOL 0x6a85028
objc[14481]: [0x6a8502c]          0x6719e40  NSObject
objc[14481]: ##############
```

The above result shows that the object is added to an autorelease pool, when the object is used via a __weak qualified variable, even without using __autoreleasing.

As a side note, _objc_rootRetainCount function does not actually return a reliable number every time. In some cases, it might return 1 even for a discarded object or invalid address. Also, if the object is used in multiple threads, the number might not be accurate because of a race condition problem.[2] Although the _objc_rootRetainCount function is helpful for debugging, be careful when using it.

Summary

In Chapter 1, we learned reference counting memory management. In Chapter 2, we learned what is changed when ARC is enabled and what rules you must follow. And, in this chapter, we learned how ARC is implemented by seeing the pseudo codes.

Now you have learned about ARC. Please take advantage of it effectively in your development on OSX and iOS.

---

[2] Wikipedia, "Race condition," http://en.wikipedia.org/wiki/Race_condition

Chapter 4

Getting Started with Blocks

Blocks are C language extensions introduced for OSX Snow Leopard, iOS4, or later. This chapter shows what Blocks are in detail so that their implementation (covered in the next chapter) will hold more meaning. Checking the implementation leads to an understanding of how to use them and how they work. To put Blocks in perspective, consider the following scenario.

When you read iOS or OSX application source code, you might find some strange sentences in it. Such sentences have function declarations inside a function. In our experience this syntax has not been found previously with C and Objective-C. The GameKit component (new in iOS4) uses the syntax quite often to make the application source code elegant. Let's see an example of it.

```
- (void)reportScore:(int64_t)score forCategory:(NSString*)category
{
        /* snip */
        [scoreReporter reportScoreWithCompletionHandler:^(NSError *error) {
                /* Tasks to be executed just after the score is reported */
            if (error != nil)
            {
                /* Tasks to be executed when an error is occurred while reporting */
            }
        }]
}
```

This example shows how to use the GameKit API to report a game score. The most important thing for users is to know whether the score has been successfully reported to the server. The application has to watch it finish and check if an error occurred. In such cases, it is very helpful for tasks to be specified to execute automatically when the reporting is done. Also it is more convenient if you can write those tasks quite easily.

In the GameKit component, you can do that by using Blocks. Blocks is where the comment, "Tasks to be executed just after the score is reported" is written in the example. This part is executed just after the reporting score is finished and not after the reportScoreWithCompletionHandler: method is called. As in the example, you don't have to monitor when the reporting is finished and you can write the tasks very elegantly by using Blocks.

In this chapter, you will learn how to use Blocks. We will start with learning what is a Block and why Blocks are needed. Then, we will learn how to use Blocks in your application, such as how to write Blocks literally and how you can use variables in the Block (as found in the source code example).

Blocks Primer

As noted, Blocks are a new extension for the C language. In short, they can be explained as "anonymous functions together with automatic (local) variables." Let's take a quick look at these two pieces and how they are implemented.

Anonymous functions

An anonymous function is, as the name suggests, a function without a name. In standard C and Objective-C, however, you can't create such functions without the help of blocks. In C++, lambda that has same concept of Blocks is finally introduced in C++11.

For example:

```
int func(int count);
```

In this source code, a function is declared with a name func. To call the function, you have to use the name "func" as follows.

```
int result = func(10);
```

You might think that you could call the function without knowing the name by using the function pointer:

```
int result = (*funcptr)(10);
```

In fact, to assign a function to the pointer, you still need its name as follows.

```
int (*funcptr)(int) = &func;
int result = (*funcptr)(10);
```

As in the examples throughout this chapter, in order to use a function, you have to name it. By using Blocks, you no longer have to do that. With Blocks, though, anonymous functions can be used. Programmers need to name so many things including functions, variables, methods, properties, classes, frameworks, and so on that it's been said that naming things is the programmer's fundamental work. So it's great that a function doesn't need its name! In the "Block Literal Syntax" section, I explain how Blocks achieve anonymous functions in detail.

Now that you know what an anonymous function is, it's important to understand what "together with automatic (local) variables" means.

Variables

Let's see which of the following variables can be used in the C language.

- Automatic variables (local variables)
- Function arguments
- Static variables (static local variables)
- Static global variables
- Global variables

Among these variable types, static, static global, and global can keep the values beyond each function call and they are stored in one memory area for the application.

In that sense, these three types are all the same except for variable scope. Even when used beyond function calls, these variables have always kept their values. In other words, the same value of the variable must be used anywhere in the application. To illustrate this, let's look at an example of a callback function for a button event.

```
int buttonId = 0;
void buttonCallback(int event)
{
    printf("buttonId:%d event=%d\n", buttonId, event);
}
```

If there is only one button in the application, this source code works fine. But how about when there are multiple buttons as follows?

```
int buttonId;
void buttonCallback(int event)
{
    printf("buttonId:%d event=%d\n", buttonId, event);
}

void setButtonCallbacks()
{
    for (int i = 0; i < BUTTON_MAX; ++i) {
        buttonId = i;
        setButtonCallback(BUTTON_IDOFFSET + i, &buttonCallback);
    }
}
```

The problem in the source code is obvious. The global variable "buttonId" is the only one and shared. All the callbacks use the same value after the for-loop. Of course, you can solve the problem by passing the button id as an argument for the callback function.

```
void buttonCallback(int buttonId, int event)     {
    printf("buttonId:%d event=%d\n", buttonId, event);
 }
```

In this case, the caller has to store not only function pointers but also button ids. By the way, in C++ and Objective-C, a class is used for this kind of situation. At first, you declare a class with a member variable and then create an object from the class to store the value in the member variable. The following source code shows how to use a class for the button callback example.

```
@interface ButtonCallbackObject : NSObject
{
    int buttonId_;
}
@end

@implementation ButtonCallbackObject
- (id) initWithButtonId:(int)buttonId
{
    self = [super init];
    buttonId_ = buttonId;
    return self;
}

- (void) callback:(int)event    {
    NSLog(@"buttonId:%d event=%d\n", buttonId_, event);
}
@end
```

The caller of the callback only has to store the object, because the class can keep the value of the button id as well.

```
void setButtonCallbacks()
{
    for (int i = 0; i < BUTTON_MAX; ++i) {
        ButtonCallbackObject *callbackObj =
            [[ButtonCallbackObject alloc] initWithButtonId:i];
        setButtonCallbackUsingObject(BUTTON_IDOFFSET, callbackObj);
    }
}
```

As you see, in C++ and Objective-C, the declaration and implementation for a class need many lines of source code. However, this can be solved with Blocks.

Blocks to the Rescue

Blocks offer features to keep variables as classes in C++ or Objective-C, with far less code. It's almost the same amount of source code as for functions. As I said "together with automatic (local) variables," Blocks hold values of auto variables. The following code shows how the previous example can be written with Blocks.

```
void setButtonCallbacks()
{
    for (int i = 0; i < BUTTON_MAX; ++i) {
        setButtonCallbackUsingBlock(BUTTON_IDOFFSET + i, ^(int event) {
            printf("buttonId:%d event=%d\n", i, event); });
    }
}
```

Its syntax is explained in the section, "Block Literal Syntax," and how automatic variables are stored is explained in the section, "Capturing automatic variables." In this source code, anonymous functions, with values of the variable "I", are set as callbacks.

With Blocks, an anonymous function is called a "Block Literal" or "Block" for short. As I said, with Blocks, you can use anonymous functions together with automatic (local) variables, meaning that Blocks can solve the problem when static (or global) variables are used, and you can have the same functionality of C++ or Objective-C classes, with far less source code.

Please note that "anonymous functions together with automatic (local) variables" is not a new idea. In fact, it is common in many languages. In computer science, it is called "Closure" or "lambda calculus." Table 4–1 shows what it is called in other languages.

Table 4–1. *Other languages' names for Block*

Programming language	The name of the feature
C+ Blocks	Block
Smalltalk	Block
Ruby	Block
LISP	Lambda
Python	Lambda
C++11	Lambda
Javascript	Anonymous function

In the following sections, we will learn how to use Blocks, starting with the syntax of Block literal.

Block Literal Syntax

This section shows how to write Block literal. The syntax of Block literal is explained with examples. After reading this, you should be able to write Block literals.

First, let's see how to declare a function in C.

```
void  func(int event) {
    printf("buttonId:%d event=%d\n", i, event);
}
```

which means it is declared by the return type, function name, argument list, and its implementation. Let's see how a Block literal is written. In previous sections, a Block literal was written in an abbreviated form as

```
^(int event) {
    printf("buttonId:%d event=%d\n", i, event);
}
```

You can also write it in full as

```
^void (int event) {
    printf("buttonId:%d event=%d\n", i, event);
}
```

There are only two differences between this Block literal and a function declaration in C: there is no function name and there is a caret symbol (^).

Block literal has no name for the function. It makes it an anonymous function. The second one means that for Block literal, a ^ (caret) is written just before the return type of the function. It is very probable that you will see this symbol more often from now on because Blocks will become common in OSX and iOS applications.

As confirmation, the following is a BNF of Block literal syntax.[1]

```
Block_literal_expression ::= ^ block_decl compound_statement_body
block_decl ::= return_type
block_decl ::= parameter_list
block_decl ::= type_expression
```

Even if you have no idea about BNF, you might be able to guess what it means. Please see Figure 4–1.

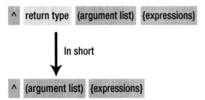

Figure 4–1. *Block literal syntax*

The return type is just same as that of a function declaration in C. The parameter list and expressions are also the same. Of course the return type has to match its "return" sentence if there is one. For example, we can use a Block literal as follows.

```
^int (int count){return count + 1;}
```

As in the previous example, some items can be omitted. First, you can omit the return type as shown in Figure 4–2.

Figure 4–2. *Block literal syntax without return type*

When the return type is omitted, the variable type in the return sentence is used instead. When the Block literal doesn't have a return sentence, "void" is used. When the Block has multiple return sentences, all of their variable types must be the same. When the return type is omitted, it is written as

```
^(int count){return count + 1;}
```

In this Block literal, the return type is int because of its return sentence.

---

[1] Wikipedia, "Backus—Naur Form" http://en.wikipedia.org/wiki/Backus-Naur_Form

If the function takes no arguments, the argument list can be omitted as well. The next source code is an example of a Block with no argument.

```
^void (void){printf("Blocks\n");}
```

This can be abbreviated as follows.

```
^{printf("Blocks\n");}
```

This abbreviated Block literal (Figure 4–3) will prove to be the most familiar form for you.

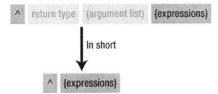

Figure 4–3. *Block literal syntax without return type and argument list*

Block type variables

As we've learned, a Block literal looks the same as a function definition except it has no name and it has the "^" symbol. For the C function, the address of the function can be assigned to a variable of the function pointer type.

```
int func(int count)
{
    return count + 1;
}
int (*funcptr)(int) = &func;
```

In the example, the address of function "func" is assigned to a variable "funcptr".

In a similar manner, a Block literal can be assigned to a Block-type variable, which means that when a Block literal is in source code, a value is generated. The value can be assigned to a variable of the Block type. In Blocks, the generated value is called Block as well. "Block" is used both for a Block literal itself in a source code and the value generated from the Block literal. Next, let's see how to declare Block-type variables.

```
int (^blk)(int);
```

If you compare the previous source code of a function pointer, you will see that the variable declaration of the Block type is the same as that of the function pointer type except for "*" and "^". Just as with normal C variable types, this declaration can be used for:

- Automatic variables
- Function arguments
- Static variables
- Static global variables
- Global variables

Next, let's see how you can assign a Block to the variable from a Block literal.

```
int (^blk)(int) = ^(int count){return count + 1;};
```

A Block is generated from the Block literal starting with "^". And the Block is assigned to the variable "blk". Of course you can assign the value to other variables of the Block type.

```
int (^blk1)(int) = blk;
```

```
int (^blk2)(int);
blk2 = blk1;
```

Functions can take arguments of Block type.

```
void func(int (^blk)(int))
{
```

Also, functions can return a Block.

```
int (^func()(int))    {
    return ^(int count){return count + 1;};
}
```

As you've seen, source code with a Block type becomes complex, especially when it is used for function arguments or its return type. You can avoid the complexity by using typedef as is done for function pointers.

```
typedef int (^blk_t)(int);
```

With this typedef, you can declare variables of "blk_t" type. So, the previous source code can be modified as follows.

```
/* original
void func(int (^blk)(int))
*/
```

```
void func(blk_t blk)
{
```

```
/* original
int (^func()(int))
*/
```

```
blk_t func()
{
```

With the typedef, the function definitions become very simple.

Incidentally, you can execute a Block, which is assigned in a variable, the same way you call a function and you can execute the Block in almost the same way as calling a function that is assigned to a variable. A variable "funcptr" of a function pointer type is called as

```
int result = (*funcptr)(10);
```

A variable "blk" of a Block type can be called as

```
int result = blk(10);
```

As you see, you can call a Block-type variable in exactly the same way as a C function. The next example shows how to execute a Block, which is passed by the argument of a function.

```
int func(blk_t blk, int rate)
{
    return blk(rate);
}
```

Of course, a Block can be used with the Objective-C method as well.

```
- (int) methodUsingBlock:(blk_t)blk rate:(int)rate     {
        return blk(rate);
}
```

You can use Block-type variables in the same way as variables in C. You can also use a pointer to Block-type variables, meaning that you can use variables of Block pointer type.

```
typedef int (^blk_t)(int);
blk_t blk = ^(int count){return count + 1;};
blk_t *blkptr = &blk;
 (*blkptr)(10);
```

Capturing automatic variables

You've learned about Block literals and Block-type variables, and should now understand the "anonymous function" part of "anonymous functions together with auto (local) variables."

Next, you need to learn what the "together with automatic (local) variables" part means. For Blocks, this can be rephrased as "capturing the value of automatic variables." The next example shows how this capture is accomplished.

```
int main()
{
    int dmy = 256;
    int val = 10;
    const char *fmt = "val = %d\n";
    void (^blk)(void) = ^{printf(fmt, val);};

    val = 2;
    fmt = "These values were changed. val = %d\n";

    blk();

    return 0;
}
```

In this source code, automatic variables "fmt" and "val" are declared and then used in the Block literal. Values of the automatic variables will be captured where the Block literal is written: the values will be stored when the Block literal is executed. Because the values have already been captured, even if they are modified after the Block literal is executed, values of the variables in the Block are never affected. In this source code, the automatic variables "fmt" and "val" are modified after the Block literal. The result is:

```
val = 10
```

It doesn't display, "These values were changed. val = 2". It displays the result with the values at the time the Block literal is executed. When it is executed, the automatic variable "fmt" has a pointer to "val = %d\n" and the "val" has integer value 10. These values are captured at that time and then used when the Block is executed.

That sums up capturing automatic variables. There is a specifier you should learn next. It is called the __block specifier. By using it, you can modify automatic variables without capturing them. The specifier is explained in the following section.

__block specifier

When automatic variables are captured, the values are read-only in the Block. The variables can't be modified. Next the source code tries to assign 1 to the automatic variable "val".

```
int val = 0;
void (^blk)(void) = ^{val = 1;};
blk();
printf("val = %d\n", val);
```

In the source code, a value is assigned to the automatic variable, which is declared outside the Block literal. This causes a compile error as follows.

```
error: variable is not assignable (missing __block type specifier)
        void (^blk)(void) = ^{val = 1;};
                              ~~~ ^
```

When an automatic variable is declared outside a Block literal, you can use __block specifier to assign a value to the variable inside the Block. The following source code uses __block specifier for the automatic variable "val" so that the variable will be assignable inside the Block.

```
__block int val = 0;
void (^blk)(void) = ^{val = 1;};
blk();
printf("val = %d\n", val);
```

The result is:

```
val = 1
```

By declaring the variable with __block specifier, you can assign values to the variable inside a Block. The __block-specified automatic variables are called "__block variables".

Captured automatic variables

As described previously, if you assign values to a captured automatic variable, a compilation error occurs.

```
int val = 0;
void (^blk)(void) = ^{val = 1;};
```

It causes the following compilation error.

```
error: variable is not assignable (missing __block type specifier)
    void (^blk)(void) = ^{val = 1;};
                          ~~~ ^
```

What happens when Objective-C objects are captured and a method is called to modify the object itself? Does it cause a compilation error as well?

```
id array = [[NSMutableArray alloc] init];
void (^blk)(void) = ^{
    id obj = [[NSObject alloc] init];
    [array addObject:obj];
};
```

No problem. An error will occur only if some value is assigned to the captured variable "array" itself. In this source code, the value of the captured variable is an object of the NS- MutableArray class. To rephrase it in C language terms, the value is a pointer to the instance of the struct for the NSMutableArray class object. If a value is assigned to the captured variable "array", a compilation error will occur.

The following source code assigns a value to the captured automatic variable, so a compilation error occurs.

```
id array = [[NSMutableArray alloc] init];
void (^blk)(void) = ^{
    array = [[NSMutableArray alloc] init];
};
```

```
error: variable is not assignable (missing __block type specifier)
    array = [[NSMutableArray alloc] init];
    ~~~~ ^
```

To do that, __block specifier is needed for the automatic variable.

```
__block id array = [[NSMutableArray alloc] init];
void (^blk)(void) = ^{
    array = [[NSMutableArray alloc] init];
};
```

One more thing. When you use a C array, you have to use a pointer intentionally. Here is an example.

```
const char text[] = "hello";

void (^blk)(void) = ^{
    printf("%c\n", text[2]);
};
```

It uses an array, which has a C string literal. Nothing is assigned to the captured automatic variable. It looks to be no problem, but it causes a compilation error as follows.

```
error: cannot refer to declaration with an array type inside block
            printf("%c\n", text[2]);
                            ^
note: declared here
        const char text[] = "hello";
                        ^
```

That is because a C array can't be captured by the current implementation of Blocks. You can avoid it by using a pointer as follows.

```
const char *text = "hello";
void (^blk)(void) = ^{
    printf("%c\n", text[2]);
};
```

Summary

In this chapter, Blocks are explained. You've learned that Blocks are "anonymous functions together with automatic (local) variables." The next chapter shows how Blocks are implemented, giving you a better understanding of their use.

Chapter 5

Blocks Implementation

In the previous chapters, we learned that a Block is an anonymous function together with automatic variables. In this chapter, we look at the details of a Block with its implementation to see what happens under the hood of Blocks. We start with the basic idea of the Block's implementation and then we show various situations to see how the Blocks work, such as how automatic variables are captured, how Blocks and __block variables are stored in memory, and how objects are captured by Blocks. Also, we show some pitfalls of Blocks related to circular reference and copy/release methods. All the example source code assumes ARC is enabled except where specified.

Under the Blocks' Hood

You might think that the Block syntax is something special. But, in reality, the compiler treats it as normal C language source code. The compiler, which supports Blocks, converts the source code with Blocks to standard C source code; then it just compiles as usual.

This is just a conceptual explanation. In reality, the compiler never generates a human-readable source code. But, clang (LLVM compiler) has a functionality to generate a human-readable converted source code.

In this section, with the converted source code, we show how the Block is implemented. The source code is bit complicated, so we delineate it step by step. First we take a glance at it, and then we go into detail.

Converting Source Code

With the "-rewrite-objc" compiler option, source code including Block syntax can be converted to standard C++ source code. Although the generated source code is in C++, it is almost always written in C except when it uses constructors for struct.

```
clang -rewrite-objc file_name_of_the_source_code
```

Let's see how the source code (Listing 5–1) is converted.

Listing 5–1. *Example with a simple Block*

```
int main()
{
    void (^blk)(void) = ^{printf("Block\n");};
    blk();
    return 0;
}
```

This source code has a Block literal in the simplest form, which has no return type and no argument list. Clang converts the source code as shown in Listing 5–2.

Listing 5–2. *Converted source code of Listing 5–1*

```
struct __block_impl {
    void *isa;
    int Flags;
    int Reserved;
    void *FuncPtr;
};

struct __main_block_impl_0 {
    struct __block_impl impl;
    struct __main_block_desc_0* Desc;

    __main_block_impl_0(void *fp, struct __main_block_desc_0 *desc, int flags=0) {
        impl.isa = &_NSConcreteStackBlock;
        impl.Flags = flags;
        impl.FuncPtr = fp;
        Desc = desc;
    }
};

static void __main_block_func_0(struct __main_block_impl_0 *__cself)
{
    printf("Block\n");
}

static struct __main_block_desc_0
{
    unsigned long reserved;
    unsigned long Block_size;
} __main_block_desc_0_DATA = {
    0,
    sizeof(struct __main_block_impl_0)
};

int main() {
    void (*blk)(void) =
        (void (*)(void))&__main_block_impl_0(
            (void *)__main_block_func_0, &__main_block_desc_0_DATA);

    ((void (*)(struct __block_impl *))(
        (struct __block_impl *)blk)->FuncPtr)((struct __block_impl *)blk);

    return 0;
}
```

It increases from 8 lines to 43 lines! But, when you look closely, you see that it isn't so complicated. We learn this step by step, starting with the Block literal in the original source code.

```
^{printf("Block\n")};
```

In the converted source code, you can see the same sentence.

```
static void __main_block_func_0(struct __main_block_impl_0 *__cself)
{
    printf("Block\n");
}
```

As shown in the converted source code, anonymous functions are converted to C functions. Function names are generated automatically and consist of a function name, where the Block literal is, and a number ordered by its appearance in the function. In the example, the function name is "main" and it is the first Block literal (0).

The argument "__cself" for the function is like "self" for the Objective-C instance method or "this" for the C++ instance method. We discuss these next.

this in C++ and self in Objective-C

In C++, an instance method for a class is defined as follows.

```
void MyClass::method(int arg)
{
    printf("%p %d\n", this, arg);
}
```

The C++ compiler converts it to a C function.

```
void __ZN7MyClass6methodEi(MyClass *this, int arg)
{
    printf("%p %d\n", this, arg);
}
```

The __ZN7MyClass6methodEi function is under the hood of the MyClass::method. An argument "this" is passed to the function. This method is called.

```
MyClass cls;
cls.method(10);
```

By the C++ compiler, it is converted to a source code calling the C function as follows.

```
struct MyClass cls;
__ZN7MyClass6methodEi(&cls, 10);
```

"this" is an instance of MyClass class (struct) itself. In addition, let's check an instance method in Objective-C.

```
- (void) method:(int)arg
{
    NSLog(@"%p %d\n", self, arg);
}
```

The same as for C++ methods, the Objective-C compiler converts the method to a C function.

```
void _I_MyObject_method_(struct MyObject *self, SEL _cmd, int arg)
{
    NSLog(@"%p %d\n", self, arg);
}
```

And the same as "this" in C++, "self" is passed as the first argument. Let's see its caller as well.

```
MyObject *obj = [[MyObject alloc] init];
[obj method:10];
```

Using "-rewrite-objc option" for clang, we can see how it is converted:

```
MyObject *obj = objc_msgSend(
    objc_getClass("MyObject"), sel_registerName("alloc"));
obj = objc_msgSend(obj, sel_registerName("init"));
objc_msgSend(obj, sel_registerName("method:"), 10);
```

The objc_msgSend function searches a pointer of the _I_MyObject_method_ function by the object and the method name. After that, it calls the function pointer, and the first argument "obj" is passed to the _I_MyObject_method_ function as its first argument "self". As in C++, "self" is the object of the MyObject class itself.

Declaring _cself

Let's continue reading the example. Unfortunately, the __main_block_func_0 function, which is converted from the Block syntax, doesn't use the argument __cself. Later, we show how __cself is used. For now, I just explain how the argument "__cself" is declared.

```
struct __main_block_impl_0 *__cself
```

Like "self" in Objective-C or "this" in C++, the argument __cself is a pointer to struct __main_block_impl_0. How is struct __main_block_impl_0 declared?

```
struct __main_block_impl_0 {
    struct __block_impl impl;
    struct __main_block_desc_0* Desc;
}
```

The converted source code is bit complex because its constructor is declared inside. After the constructor is removed, the struct __main_block_impl_0 is very simple as shown above. Next, let's check how the struct __block_impl is declared, which is used as the first member variable "impl".

```
struct __block_impl {
    void *isa;
    int Flags;
    int Reserved;
    void *FuncPtr;
};
```

From its name, we can guess what the member variable is for, such as a flag, a reserved area for a future version, and a function pointer. For now, we just skip them. First, let's see __main_block_desc_0 struct, which is used for the second member variable "Desc".

```
struct __main_block_desc_0 {
    unsigned long reserved;
    unsigned long Block_size;
};
```

As we can guess from the names, it has a reserved area and a size of a Block.

Constructor of __main_block_impl_0 struct

Next, let's check the constructor, which initializes the __main_block_impl_0 struct, which has these structs.

```
__main_block_impl_0(void *fp, struct __main_block_desc_0 *desc, int flags=0) {
    impl.isa = &_NSConcreteStackBlock;
    impl.Flags = flags;
    impl.FuncPtr = fp;
    Desc = desc;
}
```

It just initializes the member variables of __main_block_impl_0 struct. Although you might be interested in _NSConcreteStackBlock, which is used to initialize the variable "isa" in __block_impl struct that we have skipped, we first check how the constructor is called.

```
void (*blk)(void) =
    (void (*)(void))&__main_block_impl_0(
        (void *)__main_block_func_0, &__main_block_desc_0_DATA);
```

There are too many casts to understand. Just remove them all.

```
struct __main_block_impl_0 tmp =
    __main_block_impl_0(__main_block_func_0, &__main_block_desc_0_DATA);
```

```
struct __main_block_impl_0 *blk = &tmp;
```

Now, it is understandable. A pointer of an automatic variable is assigned to the variable "blk", the type of which is the pointer of __main_block_impl_0 struct. This means that an instance of __main_block_impl_0 struct is created on the stack and its pointer is assigned to the variable.

```
void (^blk)(void) = ^{printf("Block\n");};
```

The Block created from the Block literal is assigned to the Block type variable "blk". Therefore it is equivalent to assigning a pointer of an instance of __main_block_impl_0 struct to the variable "blk". The Block is equivalent to the automatic variable of __main_block_impl_0 struct type. In other words, the Block is the instance of __main_block_impl_0 struct created on the stack.

Initializing __main_block_impl_0 instance

Next, let's see how the instance of __main_block_impl_0 struct is initialized. The arguments for its constructor are:

```
__main_block_impl_0(__main_block_func_0, &__main_block_desc_0_DATA);
```

The first argument is a pointer to a function, which is converted from the Block literal. The second argument is a pointer to the instance of __main_block_desc_0 struct, which is initialized as a static global variable. Let's check how the instance of __main_block_desc_0 struct is initialized.

```
static struct __main_block_desc_0 __main_block_desc_0_DATA = {
    0,
    sizeof(struct __main_block_impl_0)
};
```

It is initialized with a size of the Block, which means a size of __main_block_impl_0 struct.

Let's see how the Block, which is the instance of __main_block_impl_0 struct on the stack, is initialized with these arguments. __main_block_impl_0 struct can be rewritten if __block_impl is expanded:

```
struct __main_block_impl_0 {
    void *isa;
    int Flags;
    int Reserved;
    void *FuncPtr;
    struct __main_block_desc_0* Desc;
}
```

This struct is initialized with the constructor as

```
isa = &_NSConcreteStackBlock;
Flags = 0;
Reserved = 0;
FuncPtr = __main_block_func_0;
Desc = &__main_block_desc_0_DATA;
```

Again, you might be interested in _NSConcreteStackBlock, however, we skip it for now. Let's check the other part first. The pointer of __main_block_func_0 function is assigned to its member "FuncPtr". It is used where

```
blk();
```

This is converted to

```
((void (*)(struct __block_impl *))(
    (struct __block_impl *)blk)->FuncPtr)((struct __block_impl *)blk);

Remove the casts again.
(*blk->impl.FuncPtr)(blk);
```

It is a simple function call via the function pointer. As we've checked, the member variable "FuncPtr" has a pointer of the __main_block_func_0 function, which is converted from the Block literal. Also, we've learned that the argument of __main_block_func_0 function "__cself" is the Block itself. With this source code, we can confirm that the Block is passed as the argument "__cself".

Reviewing _NSConcreteStackBlock

We have roughly seen what is under the hood of a Block. There is one thing that we skipped many times. What is _NSConcreteStackBlock?

```
isa = &_NSConcreteStackBlock;
```

A pointer of _NSConcreteStackBlock is assigned to a member variable "isa" in the struct for the Block. To understand what that is, we need to learn how a class and an object in Objective-C are implemented. Actually, Block is an object in Objective-C as well.

As you know, a variable type "id" is used to store an Objective-C object. We use it in Objective-C source code casually, like "void *" in C. Surprisingly, the id type is declared in C language. The declaration is in /usr/include/objc/objc.h.

```
typedef struct objc_object {
    Class isa;
} *id;
```

This means id is a pointer type of objc_object struct. Let's see what the "Class" is.

```
typedef struct objc_class *Class;
```

"Class" is a pointer type of objc_class struct. objc_class struct is declared in /usr/include/objc/runtime.h.

```
struct objc_class {
    Class isa;
};
```

It is the same as the objc_object struct. Please note that the objc_object struct and objc_class struct are used as the base struct for each object and class. Let's check that with the following simple Objective-C class declaration.

```
@interface MyObject : NSObject
{
    int val0;
    int val1;
}
@end
```

A struct for this class is based on the objc_object struct as follows.

```
struct MyObject {
    Class isa;
    int val0;
    int val1;
};
```

The instance variables "val0" and "val1" of the MyObject class are directly declared as member variables of the struct for the object. Creating an object of a class in Objective-C is equivalent to creating an instance from a struct that is generated from the class. Each created object (i.e., each instance of the struct for the object) has a pointer to the instance of the struct for its class in the member variable "isa" as shown in Figure 5–1.

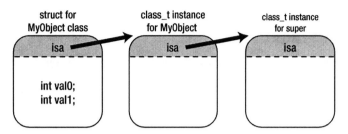

Figure 5–1. *Objective-C class and object*

A struct for each class is a class_t struct based on objc_class struct. The class_t struct is declared at runtime/objc-runtime-new.h in the objc4 runtime library.

```
struct class_t {
    struct class_t *isa;
    struct class_t *superclass;
    Cache cache;
    IMP *vtable;
    uintptr_t data_NEVER_USE;
};
```

In Objective-C, instances of class_t struct are created and stored for all the classes. For example, an instance of the class_t struct for NSObject and an instance of the class_t struct for NSMutableArray are created. These instances have the names of declared member variables, names of methods, the method implementations (which are function pointers), properties, and the pointer to its superclass. These are used by the Objective-C runtime library.

Now, we understand how a class and an object in Objective-C are implemented to go to next step. Let's check the struct for the Block again.

```
struct __main_block_impl_0 {
    void *isa;
    int Flags;
    int Reserved;
    void *FuncPtr;
    struct __main_block_desc_0* Desc;
}
```

This __main_block_impl_0 struct is based on the objc_object struct, and is a struct for Objective-C class objects. And, its member variable "isa" is initialized as follows.

```
isa = &_NSConcreteStackBlock;
```

This means that _NSConcreteStackBlock is the instance of the class_t struct. When the Block is treated as an Objective-C object, _NSConcreteStackBlock has all the information of its class. Now we've seen under the hood of Block, and we also know that a Block is an Objective-C object.

Capturing Automatic Variables

Next, let's see how capturing automatic variables is implemented. And also we discuss how the anonymous function feature is implemented. The original source code that captures automatic variables is shown in Listing 5–3.

Listing 5–3. *Capturing automatic variables*

```
int main() {
    int dmy = 256;
    int val = 10;
    const char *fmt = "val = %d\n";
    void (^blk)(void) = ^{printf(fmt, val);};
    return 0;
}
```

As we did previously, we use clang to convert the source code. The result is shown in Listing 5–4.

Listing 5–4. *Converted source code of Listing 5–3*

```
struct __main_block_impl_0 {
    struct __block_impl impl;
    struct __main_block_desc_0* Desc;
    const char *fmt;
    int val;

    __main_block_impl_0(void *fp, struct __main_block_desc_0 *desc,
            const char *_fmt, int _val, int flags=0) : fmt(_fmt), val(_val) {
        impl.isa = &_NSConcreteStackBlock;
        impl.Flags = flags;
        impl.FuncPtr = fp;
        Desc = desc;
    }
};

static void __main_block_func_0(struct __main_block_impl_0 *__cself)
{
    const char *fmt = __cself->fmt;
    int val = __cself->val;
    printf(fmt, val);
}

static struct __main_block_desc_0 {
    unsigned long reserved;
    unsigned long Block_size;
} __main_block_desc_0_DATA = {
    0,
    sizeof(struct __main_block_impl_0)
};

int main() {
    int dmy = 256;
    int val = 10;
    const char *fmt = "val = %d\n";
    void (*blk)(void) = &__main_block_impl_0(
        __main_block_func_0, &__main_block_desc_0_DATA, fmt, val);
```

```
    return 0;
}
```

Let's check the differences in the converted code from the previous example. The automatic variables used in the Block literal are added to member variables in the __main_block_impl_0 struct.

```
struct __main_block_impl_0 {
    struct __block_impl impl;
    struct __main_block_desc_0* Desc;
    const char *fmt;
    int val;
};
```

Note that only variables used by the Block are captured. In this case, "dmy" is not used, so it is not added.

```
__main_block_impl_0(void *fp, struct __main_block_desc_0 *desc,
        const char *_fmt, int _val, int flags=0) : fmt(_fmt), val(_val) {
```

When the instance of the struct is initialized, the member variables, which are added from the automatic variables, are initialized by the arguments of the constructor. Let's see what arguments are passed to the constructor.

```
void (*blk)(void) = &__main_block_impl_0(
    __main_block_func_0, &__main_block_desc_0_DATA, fmt, val);
```

The instance of __main_block_impl_0 struct is initialized with the automatic variables "fmt" and "val", which store the values at the moment when the Block literal is declared. This means that the instance of __main_block_impl_0 struct is initialized as

```
impl.isa = &_NSConcreteStackBlock;
impl.Flags = 0;
impl.FuncPtr = __main_block_func_0;
Desc = &__main_block_desc_0_DATA;
fmt = "val = %d\n";
val = 10;
```

Now we understand how the values of automatic variables are captured in the instance of __main_block_impl_0 struct, the Block.

Anonymous Function

Next, let's see the implementation of the anonymous function that uses the Block. The original Block literal is as follows.

```
^{printf(fmt, val);}
```

This is converted to a function.

```
static void __main_block_func_0(struct __main_block_impl_0 *__cself)
{
    const char *fmt = __cself->fmt;
    int val = __cself->val;
    printf(fmt, val);
}
```

In the converted source code, to make the captured automatic variables usable in this function, automatic variables are declared and defined just before the expressions generated from the Block literal. Then the original expressions in the Block literal can use the captured automatic variables in their original expressions.

To wrap up, capturing automatic variables means that when a Block literal is executed, the values of automatic variables, which are used in the Block literal, are assigned to member variables of an instance of a struct for the Block, and the instance is the Block itself.

By the way, as explained in Chapter 4, automatic variables of C array type can't be used in a Block directly. As we've learned, to capture automatic variables, the values are passed to the struct by its constructor. The following source code resembles a converted source code if a C array is used from a Block.

If a C array is passed to a constructor of a struct for a Block:

```
void func(char a[10])
{
    printf("%d\n", a[0]);
}

int main()
{
    char a[10] = {2};
    func(a);
}
```

This can be compiled and works without any problem. After that, the constructor will assign the argument to a member variable. A function, which is converted from a Block literal, assigns the member variable to an automatic variable. The source code would be as follows.

```
void func(char a[10])
{
    char b[10] = a;
    printf("%d\n", b[0]);
}

int main()
{
    char a[10] = {2};
    func(a);
}
```

This source code tries to assign a variable from a C array to a C array. It can't be compiled. Even though the type and the array length are the same, C language specification doesn't allow this kind of assignment. Of course, there are some ways to do that, but in Blocks, following C language specs seems to be considered important.

Writable Variables

Next we show how variables could be writable in Blocks. We see the two solutions to make variables writable, and start with reviewing the automatic variables that are used in Blocks. Again, see the example of capturing automatic variables (Listing 5–3).

```
^{printf(fmt, val);}
```

This source code is converted as follows.

```
static void __main_block_func_0(struct __main_block_impl_0 *__cself)
{
    const char *fmt = __cself->fmt;
    int val = __cself->val;

    printf(fmt, val);
}
```

You might have noticed something already. Only the values of the automatic variables used in the Block are captured. As I've explained, because "anonymous functions together with automatic (local) variables," after the Block use these values, they are never written back to the instance on the Block struct or to its original automatic variables.

Next the source code tries to modify the automatic variable "val" inside the Block.

```
int val = 0;
void (^blk)(void) = ^{val = 1;};
```

This causes the following compilation error.

```
error: variable is not assignable (missing __block type specifier)
    void (^blk)(void) = ^{val = 1;};
                          ~~~ ^
```

As we've learned previously, the implementation of Blocks never writes back the modified value of the variables. So, when the compiler detects an assignment to the captured automatic variable, it causes a compile error. But this limitation would be too inconvenient if you could never change the values. To solve this problem, you have two choices: using another kind of variable or using __block specifier. Let's discuss the other kind of variable first.

Static or Global Variables

In C Language, there are writable variables:

- Static variables
- Static global variables
- Global variables

An anonymous function part in a Block literal is simply converted to a C function. In the converted function, static global variables and global variables can be accessed. They work without any problem. But static variables are different. Because the converted function is declared outside the original function, where the Block literal is, static variables cannot be accessed because of the variable scope. Let's check it with the following source code.

```
int global_val = 1;
static int static_global_val = 2;

int main()
{
    static int static_val = 3;
    void (^blk)(void) = ^{
        global_val *= 1;
        static_global_val *= 2;
        static_val *= 3;
    };
    return 0;
}
```

In the Block, the static variable "static_val", static global variable "static_global_val", and global variable "global_val" are modified. How will the source code be converted?

```
int global_val = 1;
static int static_global_val = 2;

struct __main_block_impl_0 {
    struct __block_impl impl;
    struct __main_block_desc_0* Desc;
    int *static_val;
    __main_block_impl_0(void *fp, struct __main_block_desc_0 *desc,
            int *_static_val, int flags=0) : static_val(_static_val) {
        impl.isa = &_NSConcreteStackBlock;
        impl.Flags = flags;
        impl.FuncPtr = fp;
        Desc = desc;
    }
};

static void __main_block_func_0(struct __main_block_impl_0 *__cself) {
    int *static_val = __cself->static_val;

    global_val *= 1;
    static_global_val *= 2;
    (*static_val) *= 3;
}

static struct __main_block_desc_0 {
    unsigned long reserved;
    unsigned long Block_size;
} __main_block_desc_0_DATA = {
    0,
    sizeof(struct __main_block_impl_0)
};

int main()
{
    static int static_val = 3;
```

```
    blk = &__main_block_impl_0(
        __main_block_func_0, &__main_block_desc_0_DATA, &static_val);

    return 0;
}
```

The converted source code is familiar looking. The static global variable "static_global_val" and global variable "global_val" are accessed just as in the original source code. How about the static variable "static_val"? The following part shows how the variable is used inside the Block.

```
static void __main_block_func_0(struct __main_block_impl_0 *__cself) {
    int *static_val = __cself->static_val;

    (*static_val) *= 3;
}
```

The static variable "static_val" is accessed via its pointer. A pointer to the variable is passed to the constructor of _main_block_impl_0 struct, and then the constructor assigns it. This is the easiest way to use a variable beyond the variable's scope.

You might think that accessing automatic variables could be implemented in the same way as static variables. Why not? Because a Block must be able to exist even after the scope of a captured automatic variable is left. When the scope is left, the automatic variable is destroyed. Which means the Block can't access the automatic variable anymore. So, automatic variables can't be implemented the same as static variables. We learn those details in the next section.

__block specifier

As mentioned before, the other choice to avoid this problem is to use a __block specifier. To be precise, it is called a __block storage-class-specifier. In C language, the following are the storage-class-specifiers.

- typedef
- extern
- static
- auto
- register

The __block specifier is something like static, auto, and register. They specify where the variable is stored. With "auto", the value is stored on the stack as an automatic variable. With "static", the value is stored in the data section as a static variable, and so on.

Let's see how __block specifier works.

The __block specifier is used when you want to modify automatic variables from a Block, Let's use __block specifier for the previous source code, which causes a compiling error. What will happen when __block specifier is added to the automatic variable declaration?

```
__block int val = 10;
```

```
void (^blk)(void) = ^{val = 1;};
```

This source code is compiled without any problem. This is converted as shown in Listing 5–5.

Listing 5–5. *converted sourcecode that uses __block specifier*

```
struct __Block_byref_val_0 {
    void *__isa;
    __Block_byref_val_0 *__forwarding;
    int __flags;
    int __size;
    int val;
};

struct __main_block_impl_0 {
    struct __block_impl impl;
    struct __main_block_desc_0* Desc;
    __Block_byref_val_0 *val;
    __main_block_impl_0(void *fp, struct __main_block_desc_0 *desc,
            __Block_byref_val_0 *_val, int flags=0) : val(_val->__forwarding) {
        impl.isa = &_NSConcreteStackBlock;
        impl.Flags = flags;
        impl.FuncPtr = fp;
        Desc = desc;
    }
};

static void __main_block_func_0(struct __main_block_impl_0 *__cself)
{
    __Block_byref_val_0 *val = __cself->val;

    (val->__forwarding->val) = 1;
}

static void __main_block_copy_0(    struct __main_block_impl_0*dst, struct
__main_block_impl_0*src)
{
    _Block_object_assign(&dst->val, src->val, BLOCK_FIELD_IS_BYREF);
}

static void __main_block_dispose_0(struct __main_block_impl_0*src) {
    _Block_object_dispose(src->val, BLOCK_FIELD_IS_BYREF);
}

static struct __main_block_desc_0 {
    unsigned long reserved;
    unsigned long Block_size;
    void (*copy)(struct __main_block_impl_0*, struct __main_block_impl_0*);
    void (*dispose)(struct __main_block_impl_0*);
} __main_block_desc_0_DATA = {
    0,
    sizeof(struct __main_block_impl_0),
```

```
        __main_block_copy_0,
        __main_block_dispose_0
};

int main()
{
    __Block_byref_val_0 val = {
        0,
        &val,
        0,
        sizeof(__Block_byref_val_0),
        10
    };

    blk = &__main_block_impl_0(
        __main_block_func_0, &__main_block_desc_0_DATA, &val, 0x22000000);

    return 0;
}
```

When __block specifier is added for the automatic variable, the source code becomes quite large. Next, we discuss why such a large source code has to be needed only for __block specifier.

In the original source code, __block specifier was used as

```
__block int val = 10;
```

How was the __block variable "val" converted?

```
__Block_byref_val_0 val = {
    0,
     &val,
    0,
    sizeof(__Block_byref_val_0),
    10
};
```

Surprisingly, it is converted to an instance of a struct. The __block variable is an automatic variable of __Block_byref_val_0 struct, as Block is, which means that the __block variable is an instance of the __Block_byref_val_0 struct on the stack. The _block variable is initialized with 10. You can see the instance of the struct is initialized with 10, meaning that the struct stores the value of the original automatic variable in its member variable.

Let's check the declaration of the struct.

```
struct __Block_byref_val_0 {
    void *__isa;
    __Block_byref_val_0 *__forwarding;
    int __flags;
    int __size;
    int val;
};
```

As we've seen in the initializing part, the last member variable in the struct "val", stores the original automatic variable, as its name suggests.

How does the assignment to the __block variables work?

```
^{val = 1;}
```

This source code is converted as follows.

```
static void __main_block_func_0(struct __main_block_impl_0 *__cself)
{
    __Block_byref_val_0 *val = __cself->val;
    (val->__forwarding->val) = 1;
}
```

As we've learned, to assign to a static variable from a Block, a pointer to the static variable is used. Assigning to a __block variable, however, is more complicated. An instance of __main_block_impl_0 struct for the Block has a pointer to the instance of __Block_byref_val_0 struct for the __block variable.

The instance of __Block_byref_val_0 struct has a pointer to the instance of __Block_byref_val_0 struct in the member variable "__forwarding". Through the member variable "__forwarding", the member variable "val", corresponding to the original automatic variable, is accessed (Figure 5–2).

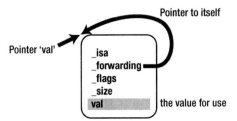

Figure 5–2. *Accessing __block variable*

We get back to "forwarding" in a bit. It is explained further in the next two sections, "Memory Segments for Blocks" and "Memory Segments for __block Variables." For now, let's look at the member variables of the __Block_byref_val_0 struct, which are not included in the __main_block_impl_0 struct. The reason why __Block_byref_val_0 struct is separated is to make the __block variable usable from more than one Block. Let's see the following example.

```
__block int val = 10;

void (^blk0)(void) = ^{val = 0;};

void (^blk1)(void) = ^{val = 1;};
```

The variables "blk0" and "blk1" of the Block type access the __block variable "val". It is converted as

```
__Block_byref_val_0 val = {0, &val, 0, sizeof(__Block_byref_val_0), 10};

blk0 = &__main_block_impl_0(
    __main_block_func_0, &__main_block_desc_0_DATA, &val, 0x22000000);
```

```
blk1 = &__main_block_impl_1(
    __main_block_func_1, &__main_block_desc_1_DATA, &val, 0x22000000);
```

Two Blocks use pointers to the same instance "val" of the __Block_byref_val_0 struct, which means that multiple Blocks can share the same __block variable. On the other hand, one Block can share multiple __block variables as well. Multiple __block variables can be used by the member variables in the struct for Block and the arguments for the constructor are just added.

Now, we've learned almost all about a __block variable. In the next section, we learn what we've skipped:

- Why can't a Block exist beyond a variable scope?

- For what does a member variable "__forwarding" of a struct for __block variables exist?

Also, in the section, "Capturing Objects," I explain the member variables "copy" and "dispose", which are added in __main_block_desc_0 struct.

Memory Segments for Blocks

In the previous sections, we've learned that a Block is implemented as an automatic variable of a struct, and the struct is generated for the Block. Also __block variable is implemented as an automatic variable of a struct, and the struct is generated for the __block variable. Because they are implemented as automatic variables of a struct, the instances are created on the stack as shown in Table 5–1.

Table 5–1. *Under the hood of Block and __block variable*

Name	Under the Hood
Block	An instance of a struct for the Block. It is created on the stack.
__block variable	An instance of a struct for __block variable. It is created on the stack.

Also, in previous sections, we've learned that a Block is an Objective-C object as well. If we see a Block as an object of Objective-C, its class is _NSConcreteStackBlock. Although not covered earlier, there are similar classes to the _NSConcreteStackBlock:

- _NSConcreteStackBlock

- _NSConcreteGlobalBlock

- _NSConcreteMallocBlock

At first, you might notice that the _NSConcreteStackBlock class has "stack" in its name, meaning that objects of this class exist on the stack. Also, objects of the _NSConcreteGlobalBlock class are, as the class name "global" shows, stored in the data section as are global variables as shown in Figure 5–3.

Objects of the _NSConcreteMallocBlock class are, as you can guess from the name, stored on the heap, like memory blocks, which are allocated by the "malloc" function.

Application's memory arrangement

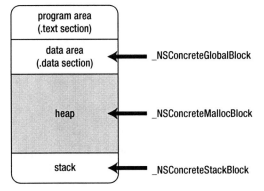

Figure 5–3. *Memory segments for Blocks*

A Block as NSConcreteGlobalBlock Class Object

The _NSConcreteStackBlock class is used for all the Blocks in the previous examples; that is, all the Blocks are stored on a stack. In the following I explain how the other class types are used.

First, when a Block literal is written where a global variable is, the Block is created as a _NSConcreteGlobalBlock class object. Let's see an example.

```
void (^blk)(void) = ^{printf("Global Block\n");};

int main()
{
```

In this source code, the Block literal is written with a global variable declaration. When it is converted, it becomes similar to the previous example in the section, "Under the Block's Hood," except that a member variable "isa" in the struct for the Block is initialized as follows.

```
impl.isa = &_NSConcreteGlobalBlock;
```

So, the class of this Block is _NSConcreteGlobalBlock, which means that an instance of a struct for the Block is stored in the data section. Because automatic variables can't exist where the global variables are declared, capturing never happens. In other words, the member variables of the instance for the Block don't rely on the execution context. One instance is enough in one application and the instance is stored in the data section as are global variables.

An instance of the struct for a Block is modified only when it captures automatic variables. For instance, in the following source code, a Block is used many times, but the automatic variable is changed and captured in every for-loop.

```
typedef int (^blk_t)(int);

for (int rate = 0; rate < 10; ++rate) {
    blk_t blk = ^(int count){return rate * count;};
}
```

The instances of the struct for the Block are different for each for-loop because they capture the automatic variable. But, if the Block doesn't capture any variables, the instance of the struct for the Block is the same:

```
typedef int (^blk_t)(int);

for (int rate = 0; rate < 10; ++rate) {
    blk_t blk = ^(int count){return count;};
}
```

The instance of the struct for the Block is stored in the data section of the program not only when Block is used where there are global variables, but also when a Block literal is inside a function and doesn't capture any automatic variables.

In the converted source code with clang, _NSConcreteStackBlock class is always used, but the implementation is different. We can summarize it as follows.

- When a Block literal is written where there are global variables

- When the syntax in a Block literal doesn't use any automatic variables to be captured

In these cases, the Block will be a _NSConcreteGlobalBlock class object and is stored in the data section. Any Block created by another kind of Block literal will be an object of the _NSConcreteStackBlock class, and be stored on the stack.

When is the _NSConcreteMallocBlock class used and the Block stored on the heap? This is the exact answer for the questions in the previous section.

- Why can't a Block exist beyond a variable scope?

- Why does a member variable "__forwarding" of a struct for __block variables exist?

A Block, which is stored in the data section like global variables, can be accessed safely via pointers outside any variable scopes. But the other Blocks, which are stored on the stack, will be disposed of after the scope of the Block is left. And __block variables are stored on the stack as well, so the __block variables will be disposed of when the scope is left (Figure 5–4).

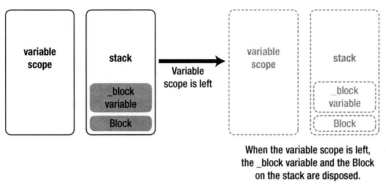

When the variable scope is left,
the _block variable and the Block
on the stack are disposed.

Figure 5–4. *A Block and a __block variable on the stack*

To solve this problem, Blocks provides a functionality to copy a Block or a __block variable from the stack to the heap. Next, we learn how a Block is copied to the heap.

Block on the Heap

As we've learned, a Block can be copied to the heap. By copying the Block, the copied Block on the heap can exist even after the scope is left as shown in Figure 5–5. Let's see what tricks there are to having the Block work properly.

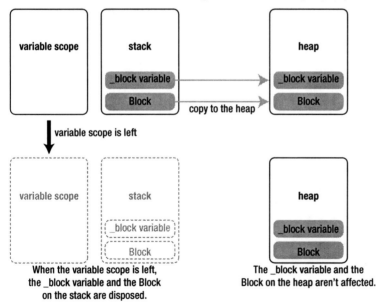

When the variable scope is left,
the _block variable and the Block
on the stack are disposed.

The _block variable and the
Block on the heap aren't affected.

Figure 5–5. *A Block and __block copied from the stack to the heap*

The member variable "isa" of the struct for the copied Block on the heap is overwritten so that the Block becomes a _NSConcreteMallocBlock class object.

```
impl.isa = &_NSConcreteMallocBlock;
```

Meanwhile, a __block variable must be accessed properly no matter where it is on the stack or the heap. The member variable "__forwarding" in the struct for a __block variable is used for that.

Even if a __block variable has been copied to the heap, the __block variable on the stack is still accessed in some cases. Because the member variable "__forwarding" of the instance on the stack points to the instance on the heap, regardless of where the __block variable is on the stack or heap, it is accessed properly. I explain this again in the section, "Memory Segments for __Block Variables."

Copying Blocks Automatically

By the way, how do Blocks offer copy functionality? To tell the truth, when ARC-enabled, in many cases the compiler automatically detects and copies the Block from the stack to the heap. Let's see the next example, which calls a function returning a Block.

```
typedef int (^blk_t)(int);

blk_t func(int rate)
{
    return ^(int count){return rate * count;};
}
```

A function returns a Block, which is stored on the stack; that is, when the control flow returns to the caller, the variable scope is left and the Block on the stack is disposed of. It looks problematic. Let's check how it is converted when ARC is enabled.

```
blk_t func(int rate)
{
    blk_t tmp = &__func_block_impl_0(
        __func_block_func_0, &__func_block_desc_0_DATA, rate);

    tmp = objc_retainBlock(tmp);

    return objc_autoreleaseReturnValue(tmp);
}
```

Because ARC is enabled, "blk_t tmp" is same as "blk_t __strong tmp", which means the variable is qualified with __strong.

If you'd read the source code runtime/objc-arr.mm in the objc4 runtime library, you saw that objc_retainBlock function is equivalent to _Block_copy function. So, the above source code is equivalent to:

```
tmp = _Block_copy(tmp);

return objc_autoreleaseReturnValue(tmp);
```

Let's see what happens with comments:

```
/*
 * a Block is assigned from a Block literal to a variable 'tmp',
 * which means, the variable has the instance of struct for the Block on the stack.
 * Block_copy function copies the Block from the stack to the heap.
```

```
 * After it is copied, its address on the heap is assigned to the variable 'tmp'.
 */

tmp = _Block_copy(tmp);

 /*
 * Then, the Block on the heap is registered to an autoreleasepool as an Objective-C
object.
 * After that, the Block is returned.
 */

return objc_autoreleaseReturnValue(tmp);
```

This means when the function returns the Block, the compiler automatically copies it to the heap.

Coping Blocks Manually

I've stated that "in many cases, the compiler automatically detects." When it doesn't detect, you have to copy the Block from the stack to the heap manually. To do that, you use an instance method "copy". The "copy" method, which we've seen many times in Part I, is in the alloc/new/copy/mutableCopy method group. In what situation can't the compiler detect it?

The answer is:

▓   When a Block is passed as an argument for methods or functions

But if the method or the function copies the argument inside, the caller doesn't need to copy it manually as

▓   Cocoa Framework methods, the name of which includes "usingBlock"

▓   Grand Central Dispatch API

For example, you don't need to copy when you use the NSArray instance method "enumerateOb- jectsUsingBlock" or "dispatch_async" function. On the contrary, you need to copy a Block when you pass it to an NSArray class instance method "initWithObjects". Let's see that with an example.

```
- (id) getBlockArray
{
    int val = 10;

    return [[NSArray alloc] initWithObjects:
        ^{NSLog(@"blk0:%d", val);},
        ^{NSLog(@"blk1:%d", val);}, nil];
}
```

The "getBlockArray" method creates two Blocks on the stack and it passes them to the NSArray class instance method "initWithObjects". What happens when the Block is executed in the caller after the Block is obtained from the NSArray object?

```
id obj = getBlockArray();

typedef void (^blk_t)(void);

blk_t blk = (blk_t)[obj objectAtIndex:0];

blk();
```

The application crashes where "blk()" is executed. In other words, Block execution throws an exception. After returning from the getBlockArray function, the Block on the stack has been destroyed. In this case, unfortunately, the compiler can't detect whether a copy is needed. Although the compiler could copy all the Blocks every time without detecting if a copy is needed, it consumes too many CPU resources when a Block is copied from the stack to the heap. If a Block on the stack is enough and still copied to the heap, CPU power is just being used for nothing. So, the compiler doesn't do that. But, instead, sometimes you have to copy a Block manually.

The source code will work after some modifications as follows.

```
- (id) getBlockArray
{
    int val = 10;

    return [[NSArray alloc] initWithObjects:
        [^{NSLog(@"blk0:%d", val);} copy],
        [^{NSLog(@"blk1:%d", val);} copy], nil];
}
```

It looks a bit strange, but the "copy" method can be called on a Block literal directly. Of course you can call the "copy" method through a Block type variable.

```
typedef int (^blk_t)(int);

blk_t blk = ^(int count){return rate * count;};

blk = [blk copy];
```

By the way, what will happen if the "copy" method is called on a Block on the heap or on a data section? Table 5–2 summarizes them.

Table 5–2. *Block copy*

Block Class	Copied From	How "Copy" Works
_NSConcreteStackBlock	Stack	Copy from the stack to the heap
_NSConcreteGlobalBlock	.data section of the program	Do nothing
_NSConcreteMallocBlock	Heap	Increment the reference count of the object

No matter where the Block is stored, nothing bad happens by calling the copy method. If you are not sure if you have to copy, it is safe just to call "copy" on the Block.

But, is it all right to call "copy" multiple times? With ARC, we can't call release, however.

Copying Block Multiple Times

```
blk = [[[[blk copy] copy] copy] copy];
```

This can be rewritten as follows.

```
{
    blk_t tmp = [blk copy];
    blk = tmp;
}
{
    blk_t tmp = [blk copy];
    blk = tmp;
}
{
    blk_t tmp = [blk copy];
    blk = tmp;
}
{
    blk_t tmp = [blk copy];
    blk = tmp;
}
```

Let's check the source code with comments as shown in Listing 5–6.

Listing 5–6. *Copying multiple times with comments*

```
    /*
     * Assume that a Block on the stack was assigned to the variable 'blk'
     */

    blk_t tmp = [blk copy];

    /*
     * A Block on the heap is assigned to the variable 'tmp'.
     * 'tmp' has ownership of it because of its strong reference.
     */

    blk = tmp;

    /*
     * The Block in the variable 'tmp' is assigned to the variable 'blk'.
     * 'blk' has ownership of it because of its strong reference.
     *
     * The Block, which was originally assigned to 'blk',
     * is not affected by this assignment, because it is on the stack.
     *
     * At this moment, the variables 'blk' and 'tmp' have ownership of the Block.
     */

}
    /*
     * Leaving the variable scope 'tmp',
     * and its strong reference disappears and the Block is released.
     *
```

```
     * Because the variable 'blk' has ownership of it, the Block isn't disposed of.
     */
{
    /*
     * The variable 'blk' has the Block on the heap.
     * 'blk' has ownership of it because of its strong reference.
     */

    blk_t tmp = [blk copy];

    /*
     * A Block on the heap is assigned to the variable 'tmp'.
     * 'tmp' has ownership of it because of its strong reference.
     */

    blk = tmp;

    /*
     * Because the different value is assigned to the variable 'blk',
     * The strong reference to the Block, which was assigned in the variable 'blk',
disappears
     * and the Block is released.
     *
     * The variable 'tmp' has ownership of the Block,
     * The Block isn't disposed of.
     *
     * The Block in the variable 'tmp' is assigned to the variable 'blk'.
     * The variable 'blk' has ownership because of the strong reference.
     *
     * At this moment, the variables 'blk' and 'tmp' have ownership of the Block.
     */

}
    /*
     * Leaving the variable scope 'tmp',
     * and its strong reference disappears and the Block is released.
     *
     * Because the variable 'blk' has ownership of it, the Block isn't disposed of.
     */

    /*
     * repeating ...
     */
```

With ARC, it works with no problem.

Memory Segments for __block Variables

In the previous section, we've learned only about Blocks. How about __block variables?
When a Block uses a __block variable and is copied from the stack to the heap, the
__block variable is affected. Table 5–3 summarizes that.

Table 5–3. *__block variables when Block is copied from the stack to the heap.*

Storage of __block Variable	When a Block Is Copied from the Stack to the Heap
Stack	The __block variable is copied from the stack to the heap. The Block will have ownership of it.
Heap	The Block has ownership of the __block variable.

When a Block is copied from the stack to the heap and it uses __block variables and the __block variables aren't used in the other Blocks, the __block variables must be on the stack. And, at the moment, all the __block variables are also copied from the stack to the heap and the Block has ownership of the __block variables as shown in Figure 5–6.

When the Block on the heap is copied again, the __block variables will not be affected.

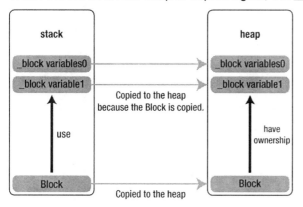

Figure 5–6. *A Block uses __block variables*

What will happen if __block variables are used from more than one Block? At the beginning, all the Blocks and the __block variables are on the stack. When one of the Blocks is copied from the stack to the heap, the __block variables are copied from the stack to the heap. And the Block has ownership of the variables. When another Block is copied from the stack to the heap, the copied Block has ownership of the __block variables (Figure 5–7). In other words, the reference count of the __block variables is +1.

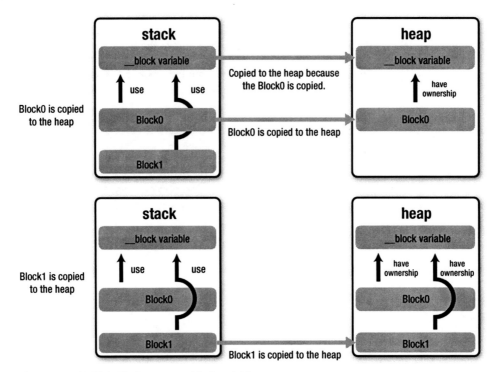

Figure 5–7. *Multiple Blocks uses a __block variable*

When a Block on the heap is disposed of, __block variables, which are used in the Block, are released as shown in Figure 5–8.

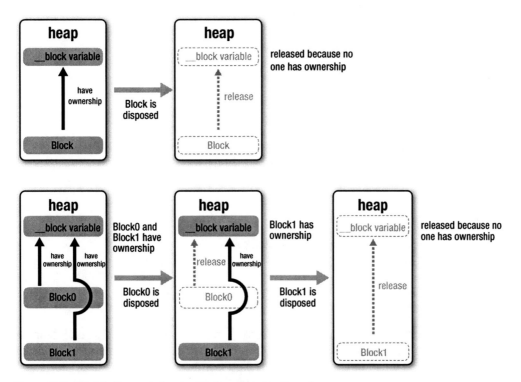

Figure 5–8. *Block is disposed of and __block variable is released*

This concept is exactly the same as memory management with reference counting in Objective-C. The Block has ownership of the __block variables when the Block uses it. When the Block is disposed of, the ownership disappears and the __block variables are released.

Now we've learned how __block variables are stored on application memory. Let's move on to _forwarding.

__forwarding

__forwarding is used to access __block variables properly as I explained in the section, "Memory Segments for Blocks." Next, let's check how it works when a Block is copied to the heap.

I've explained that the member variable "__forwarding" of the instance on the stack has the pointer to the instance on the heap so that the variable is accessed properly no matter where it is on the stack or on the heap.

A __block variable is copied from the stack to the heap when a Block is copied as well. In this situation, both the __block variables on the stack and on the heap might be accessed at the same time. Let's see the following example.

```
__block int val = 0;
```

```
 void (^blk)(void) = [^{++val;} copy];
```

```
++val;
```

```
blk();
```

```
NSLog(@"%d", val);
```

When the Block using a __block variable is copied by the "copy" method, not only the Block but also the __block variable is copied from the stack to the heap.

Let's see where the __block variable is used. After it is initialized, it is used inside the Block literal.

```
^{++val;}
```

After the Block literal, it is used outside the Block as well:

```
++val;
```

Both source codes are converted in the same way as follows.

```
++(val.__forwarding->val);
```

In the function, which is converted from the Block literal, the variable "val" is an instance of the struct for __block variable on the heap. The other variable "val" outside the Block is on the stack. When the __block variable is copied from the stack to the heap, the member variable "__forwarding" of the instance on the stack is modified to the address of the copied instance on the heap as shown in Figure 5–9.

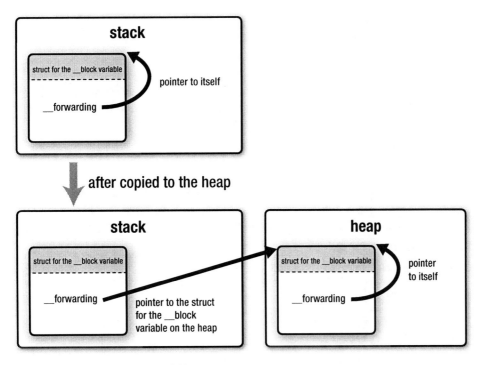

Figure 5–9. *Copying a __block variable*

With this mechanism, we can access the same __block variable from anywhere, inside the Block literal or outside Block literal, no matter where the __block variable is on the stack or on the heap.

Capturing Objects

We saw examples using integer variables. Next, let's see what will happen when an object is used from a Block. In the next source code, an object of the NSMutableArray class is created and the assigned variable has ownership of it. Because the scope of the variable, which qualified with __strong, is left immediately, the object is released and discarded.

```
{
    id array = [[NSMutableArray alloc] init];
}
```

Listing 5–7 uses the variable "array" in a Block literal.

Listing 5–7. *Capturing an object*

```
blk_t blk;
{
    id array = [[NSMutableArray alloc] init];
    blk = [^(id obj) {
        [array addObject:obj];
        NSLog(@"array count = %ld", [array count]);
    } copy];
}
```

```
    }
    blk([[NSObject alloc] init]);
    blk([[NSObject alloc] init]);

    blk([[NSObject alloc] init]);
```

Because the strong reference of variable "array" disappears, the NSMutableArray class object, which is assigned to the variable "array", must be released and discarded. But the result shows that it works without any problem.

```
array count = 1
array count = 2
array count = 3
```

This means that in the last part of the source code, where the Block is executed, the object of NSMutableArray class, which is assigned to the variable "array", exists even after the variable scope is finished. The source code is converted as shown in Listing 5–8.

Listing 5–8. *Converted source code of Listing 5–7*

```
/* a struct for the Block and some functions */

struct __main_block_impl_0 {
    struct __block_impl impl;
    struct __main_block_desc_0* Desc;
    id __strong array;
    __main_block_impl_0(void *fp, struct __main_block_desc_0 *desc,
    id __strong _array, int flags=0) : array(_array) {
        impl.isa = &_NSConcreteStackBlock;
        impl.Flags = flags;
        impl.FuncPtr = fp;
        Desc = desc;
    }
};

static void __main_block_func_0(struct __main_block_impl_0 *__cself, id obj)
{
    id __strong array = __cself->array;
    [array addObject:obj];
    NSLog(@"array count = %ld", [array count]);
}

static void __main_block_copy_0(struct __main_block_impl_0 *dst,          struct
__main_block_impl_0 *src)
{
    _Block_object_assign(&dst->array, src->array, BLOCK_FIELD_IS_OBJECT);
}

static void __main_block_dispose_0(struct __main_block_impl_0 *src)
{
    _Block_object_dispose(src->array, BLOCK_FIELD_IS_OBJECT);
}

static struct __main_block_desc_0 {
    unsigned long reserved;
    unsigned long Block_size;
    void (*copy)(struct __main_block_impl_0*, struct __main_block_impl_0*);
    void (*dispose)(struct __main_block_impl_0*);
```

```
} __main_block_desc_0_DATA = {
    0,
    sizeof(struct __main_block_impl_0),
    __main_block_copy_0,
    __main_block_dispose_0
};
```

```
/* Block literal and executing the Block */
```

```
blk_t blk;
{
    id __strong array = [[NSMutableArray alloc] init];

    blk = &__main_block_impl_0(
        __main_block_func_0, &__main_block_desc_0_DATA, array, 0x22000000);
    blk = [blk copy];
}
```

```
(*blk->impl.FuncPtr)(blk, [[NSObject alloc] init]);
(*blk->impl.FuncPtr)(blk, [[NSObject alloc] init]);
(*blk->impl.FuncPtr)(blk, [[NSObject alloc] init]);
```

Please pay attention to the captured automatic variable "array" which stores the object of the NSMutableArray class. You can see that the struct for the Block has a member variable "array" with __strong ownership qualifier.

```
struct __main_block_impl_0 {
    struct __block_impl impl;
    struct __main_block_desc_0* Desc;
    id __strong array;
};
```

In Objective-C, the C struct cannot have member variables that are qualified with __strong as we learned in Chapter 2. The reason is that the compiler can't detect when the C struct is initialized or discarded in order to do proper memory management.

However, the Objective-C runtime library can detect when a Block is copied from the stack to the heap, and when a Block on the heap is destroyed. So, if the struct for Block has variables that are qualified with __strong or __weak, the compiler can initialize and dispose of them properly. For that, the member variables in struct __main_block_desc_0 "copy" and "dispose" are added and functions __main_block_copy_0 and __main_block_dispose_0 are assigned to them.

In the source code, the struct for the Block has an object type variable "array", which is qualified with __strong. Because the compiler has to manage the object in the variable "array" properly, the __main_block_copy_0 function calls the _Block_object_assign function to assign the target object to the member variable "array" and to take ownership of it.

```
static void __main_block_copy_0(struct __main_block_impl_0 *dst,
        struct __main_block_impl_0 *src)
{
    _Block_object_assign(&dst->array, src->array, BLOCK_FIELD_IS_OBJECT);
}
```

The _Block_object_assign function assigns the object to the member variable and calls a function, which is equivalent to the retain method.

Also, the __main_block_dispose_0 function calls the _Block_object_dispose function to release the object, which is assigned to the member variable "array" in the struct for the Block.

```
static void __main_block_dispose_0(struct __main_block_impl_0 *src)
{
    _Block_object_dispose(src->array, BLOCK_FIELD_IS_OBJECT);
}
```

The _Block_object_dispose function calls a function, which is equivalent to the instance method "release", on the object in the target member variable of the struct.

By the way, the __main_block_copy_0 function (referred to as "copy function" in the rest of this book) and the __main_block_dispose_0 function (dispose function) are assigned to the member variables "copy" and "dispose" in the __main_block_desc_0 struct. But in the converted source code, none of these functions are called at all, including through the pointers. How are the functions used?

These functions are called when the Block is copied from the stack to the heap, and when the Block on the heap is disposed of (see Table 5–4).

Table 5–4. *When the copy function and dispose function are called*

Function	When It Is Called
copy function	When the Block on the stack is copied to the heap
dispose function	When the Block on the heap is discarded

When is the Block on the stack copied to the heap?

- When the instance method "copy" is called on the Block

- When the Block is returned from a function

- When the Block is assigned to a member variable of id or the Block type class, with __strong qualifier

- When the Block is passed to a method, including "usingBlock" in the Cocoa Framework, or a Grand Central Dispatch API

"When the instance method 'copy' is called on the Block," if the Block is on the stack, the Block is copied to the heap. "When the Block is returned from a function" or "When the Block is assigned to a member variable of id or the Block type class, with __strong qualifier," the compiler automatically calls the _Block_copy function with the target Block as an argument, which is equivalent to calling a "copy" instance method on the Block. "When the Block is passed to a method, including 'usingBlock' in the Cocoa Framework, or a Grand Central Dispatch API," the instance method "copy" is called on the Block or the _Block_copy function is called with the Block as the argument inside the method or function.

A Block on the stack will be copied that way in the various situations, but, in a sense, all the situations are just the same. Actually, a Block is copied only when the _Block_copy function is called.

On the contrary, the dispose function is called when a Block on the heap is released and disposed of because no one has ownership of it. It is equivalent to the dealloc method of objects. With this mechanism, the object, which is captured by a Block, can exist beyond the variable scope by assigning to an automatic variable with a __strong qualifier. Although we skipped it in the section "__block specifier," this mechanism with copy and dispose functions is used for __block variables as well.

```
static void __main_block_copy_0(
    struct __main_block_impl_0*dst, struct __main_block_impl_0*src)
{
    _Block_object_assign(&dst->val, src->val, BLOCK_FIELD_IS_BYREF);
}

static void __main_block_dispose_0(struct __main_block_impl_0*src) {
    _Block_object_dispose(src->val, BLOCK_FIELD_IS_BYREF);
}
```

In the converted source code, a portion related to the struct for the Block is almost the same except for the difference listed in Table 5–5.

Table 5–5. *Difference when an object is captured and when __block variable is used*

type	Argument
Object	BLOCK_FIELD_IS_OBJECT
__block variable	BLOCK_FIELD_IS_BYREF

The argument BLOCK_FIELD_IS_OBJECT and BLOCK_FIELD_IS_BYREF switches the target of copy and dispose functions over the object or the __block variable.

The same way it takes ownership of the captured object by the copy function and the ownership is released by the dispose function, it takes ownership of the __block variable by the copy function and the ownership is released by the dispose function.

Now we've learned that when an object is assigned to automatic variables with __strong, the object can exist beyond the variable scope, and when a __block variable is copied to the heap and a Block on the heap has ownership of it, it can exist beyond the variable scope.

When You Should Call the "copy" Method

By the way, in the previous source code, what will happen when the instance method "copy" isn't called on the Block?

```
blk_t blk;

{
```

```
        id array = [[NSMutableArray alloc] init];
        blk = ^(id obj) {
            [array addObject:obj];
            NSLog(@"array count = %ld", [array count]);
        };
    }

blk([[NSObject alloc] init]);
blk([[NSObject alloc] init]);
blk([[NSObject alloc] init]);
```

As the result, the application is terminated.

Only when the _Block_copy function is called, is ownership of the captured object type automatic variable with a __strong qualifier taken. So, as an example, if the _Block_copy function isn't called, the object is disposed of even if the object is captured. Therefore, when you use an automatic variable of an object type inside a Block, you should call the instance method "copy" on the Block, except in the following situations.

- ■ When the Block is returned from a function

- ■ When the Block is assigned to a member variable of id or the Block type class, with a __strong qualifier

- ■ When the Block is passed to a method, including "usingBlock" in the Cocoa Framework, or a Grand Central Dispatch API

Next, let's see what happens when an object is stored in a __block variable.

__block Variables and Objects

The __block specifier can be used for any type of automatic variable. Let's see how it is used for an id-type automatic variable to assign an Objective-C object.

```
__block id obj = [[NSObject alloc] init];
```

This is equivalent to:

```
__block id __strong obj = [[NSObject alloc] init];
```

When ARC is enabled, variables of id or an object type always have ownership qualifiers, and __strong is used as its default. It is converted by clang as follows.

```
/* struct for __block variable */

struct __Block_byref_obj_0 {
    void *__isa;
    __Block_byref_obj_0 *__forwarding;
    int __flags;
    int __size;
    void (*__Block_byref_id_object_copy)(void*, void*);
    void (*__Block_byref_id_object_dispose)(void*);
    __strong id obj;
};

static void __Block_byref_id_object_copy_131(void *dst, void *src) {
```

```
        _Block_object_assign((char*)dst + 40, *(void * *) ((char*)src + 40), 131);
}

static void __Block_byref_id_object_dispose_131(void *src) {
        _Block_object_dispose(*(void * *) ((char*)src + 40), 131);
}


/* __block variable declaration */

  __Block_byref_obj_0 obj = {
        0,
        &obj,
        0x2000000,
        sizeof(__Block_byref_obj_0),
        __Block_byref_id_object_copy_131,
        __Block_byref_id_object_dispose_131,
        [[NSObject alloc] init]
};
```

_Block_object_assign and _Block_object_dispose functions, which are explained in the previous section, are used.

When an automatic variable of id or object type is captured for a Block and the Block is copied from the stack to the heap, the _Block_object_assign function is called so that the Block takes ownership of the captured object. When the block on the heap is disposed of, the _Block_object_dispose function is called to release the captured object.

When an automatic variable of id or object type with a __strong qualifier has a __block specifier, the same thing happens. When the __block variable is copied from the stack to the heap, a _Block_object_assign function is called so that the Block takes ownership of the __block variable. When the __block variable on the heap is disposed of, the _Block_object_dispose function is called to release the object in the __block variable.

Now we understand that as long as the object type __block variable with a __strong qualifier exists on the heap, the object, which is assigned to the __block variable, exists as well and ownership of it is managed properly. It is just like an object, which is assigned to the object type automatic variable with a __strong qualifier, is used inside a Block.

By the way, for now, we've learned only about automatic variables of id or object type with a __strong qualifier. How about other ownership qualifiers? What will happen with __weak ownership qualifiers? The next source code is about id type variables with a __weak qualifier.

```
blk_t blk;

{
    id array = [[NSMutableArray alloc] init];
    id __weak array2 = array;
    blk = [^(id obj) {

        [array2 addObject:obj];

        NSLog(@"array2 count = %ld", [array2 count]);
```

```
    } copy];
}
```

```
blk([[NSObject alloc] init]);
blk([[NSObject alloc] init]);
blk([[NSObject alloc] init]);
```

The result is different from the result in the section, "Capturing Objects."

```
array2 count = 0
array2 count = 0
array2 count = 0
```

This is because the variable "array" is released and discarded when the variable scope is left, and nil is assigned to the variable "array2". It just works as expected.

What will happen when the __block specifier and __weak ownership qualifier are used at the same time?

```
blk_t blk;

{
    id array = [[NSMutableArray alloc] init];
    __block id __weak array2 = array;

    blk = [^(id obj) {

        [array2 addObject:obj];

        NSLog(@"array2 count = %ld", [array2 count]);
    } copy];
}
```

```
blk([[NSObject alloc] init]);
blk([[NSObject alloc] init]);
blk([[NSObject alloc] init]);
```

The result is same as the previous one.

```
array2 count = 0
array2 count = 0
array2 count = 0
```

Even with __block specifier, when the variable scope is left, the variable "array" with a __strong qualifier is released and discarded, and then nil is assigned to the variable "array2" because "array2" is qualified with __weak.

A variable with a __unsafe_unretained qualifier is just same as a simple pointer. No matter how it is used, inside a Block or with a __block specifier, no mechanism for a __strong or __weak qualifier works. So, when you use a variable with __unsafe_unretained qualifier, please take care not to access a discarded object through the dangling pointer. Please see Chapter 2, the "__unsafe_unretained ownership qualifier" section.

The __autoreleasing qualifier is not assumed to be used with a Block, and so it should not be used. If you use it with __block specifier, a compiling error occurs.

```
__block id __autoreleasing obj = [[NSObject alloc] init];
```

Because the __autoreleasing ownership qualifier and __block specifier are used for the variable "obj", a compiling error occurs:

```
error: __block variables cannot have __autoreleasing ownership
    __block id __autoreleasing obj = [[NSObject alloc] init];
                                     ^
```

Circular Reference with Blocks

If a Block uses an automatic variable of object type with a __strong qualifier, when the Block is copied from the stack to the heap, the Block has the ownership of the object. It easily causes circular reference. Let's see the next example.

```
typedef void (^blk_t)(void);

@interface MyObject : NSObject
{
    blk_t blk_;
}
@end

@implementation MyObject

- (id)init
{
    self = [super init];
    blk_ = ^{NSLog(@"self = %@", self);};
    return self;
}

- (void)dealloc
{
    NSLog(@"dealloc");
}
@end

int main()
{
    id o = [[MyObject alloc] init];
    NSLog(@"%@", o);
    return 0;
}
```

In this example, the instance method "dealloc" of MyObject class is never called.

The object of MyObject class has a strong reference to a Block, which is assigned to the Block type member variable "blk_", meaning that the object of MyObject class has the ownership of the Block. The Block literal is executed in the instance method "init", and it uses the id-type variable "self" with a __strong qualifier. When the Block literal is assigned to the member variable "blk_", the Block, which is generated by the Block literal, is copied from the stack to the heap. The Block has ownership of "self", because the Block uses "self".

So, "self" has ownership of the Block and the Block has ownership of "self". This is a circular reference as shown in Figure 5–10.

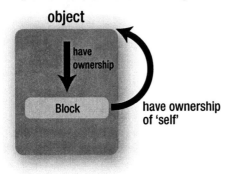

Figure 5–10. *Circular reference with a Block member variable*

In this case, the compiler can detect the circular reference. The warning message is displayed properly.

```
warning: capturing 'self' strongly in this block is likely to lead
         to a retain cycle [-Warc-retain-cycles]
              blk_ = ^{NSLog(@"self = %@", self);};
                                            ^~~~
```

```
note: Block will be retained by an object strongly retained by the
      captured object
           blk_ = ^{NSLog(@"self = %@", self);};
           ^~~~
```

To avoid the circular reference, for instance, you can declare the variable with __weak qualifier and assign "self" to it (Figure 5–11).

```
- (id)init
{
    self = [super init];
    id __weak tmp = self;
    blk_ = ^{NSLog(@"self = %@", tmp);};
    return self;
}
```

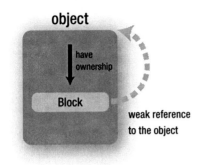

Figure 5–11. *Avoiding circular reference of a Block member variable*

In the source code, as long as the Block exists, the object of MyObject class, which has ownership of the Block, exists as well, meaning that self, which is assigned to the variable "tmp" always exists. So, you don't need to check if "tmp" is nil or not.

For iOS4 or Snow Leopard applications, you have to use the __unsafe_unretained ownership qualifier instead of __weak. You can use it without worrying about a dangling pointer for this example.

```
- (id)init {
    self = [super init];
    id __unsafe_unretained tmp = self;
    blk_ = ^{NSLog(@"self = %@", tmp);};
    return self;
}
```

And, in the next source code, circular reference occurs because self is captured even though self isn't used in the Block.

```
@interface MyObject : NSObject
{
    blk_t blk_;
    id obj_;
}
@end

@implementation MyObject
- (id)init
{
    self = [super init];
    blk_ = ^{NSLog(@"obj_ = %@", obj_);};
    return self;
}
```

You can discover the reason from the warning message:

```
warning: capturing 'self' strongly in this Block is likely to lead
        to a retain cycle [-Warc-retain-cycles]
            blk_ = ^{NSLog(@"obj_ = %@", obj_);};
                                            ^~~~
note: Block will be retained by an object strongly retained by the
        captured object
            blk_ = ^{NSLog(@"obj_ = %@", obj_);};
```

```
                    ^~~~
```

Because the Block literal uses "obj_", self is captured. In fact, for the compiler, "obj_" is just a member variable of the struct for the object as follows.

```
blk_ = ^{NSLog(@"obj_ = %@", self->obj_);};
```

You can avoid the circular reference using a __weak ownership qualifier for "obj_" as for the previous example. In this example, you can use a __unsafe_unretained ownership qualifier safely as well for the same reason.

```
- (id)init
{
    self = [super init];
    id __weak obj = obj_;
    blk_ = ^{NSLog(@"obj_ = %@", obj);};
    return self;
}
```

When you use a __weak ownership qualifier to avoid circular reference, even though you can check whether the variable is nil to know that the object exists, the object should exist the entire time you use the variable.

Also, there is another way to avoid a circular reference. You can do that by using __block variable as follows.

```
typedef void (^blk_t)(void);

@interface MyObject : NSObject
{
    blk_t blk_;
}
@end

@implementation MyObject

- (id)init
{
    self = [super init];
    __block id tmp = self;
    blk_ = ^{
        NSLog(@"self = %@", tmp);
        tmp = nil;
    };
    return self;
}

- (void)execBlock
{
    blk_();
}

- (void)dealloc
{
    NSLog(@"dealloc");
}
@end
```

```
int main()
{
    id o = [[MyObject alloc] init];
    [o execBlock];
    return 0;
}
```

This source code doesn't cause a circular reference. However, if you don't call the instance method "execBlock", in other words, if the Block assigned to the member variable "blk_" isn't executed, a circular reference will occur as in Figure 5–12.

After the object of the MyObject class is created, circular reference exists there because:

■ The object of MyObject class has ownership of the Block.

■ The Block has ownership of the __block variable.

■ The __block variable has ownership of the MyObject class object.

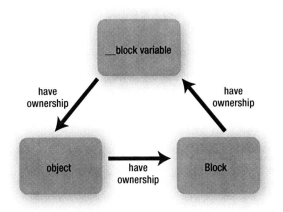

Figure 5–12. *Circular reference*

If the instance method "execBlock" isn't called, the circular reference causes a memory leak. By calling the instance method "execBlock", the Block is executed and nil is assigned to the __block variable "tmp".

```
blk_ = ^{
    NSLog(@"self = %@", tmp);
    tmp = nil;
};
```

After that the __block variable "tmp" doesn't have the strong reference to the MyObject class object anymore. So, the circular reference disappears as shown in Figure 5–13. The relationship is:

■ The object of MyObject class has ownership of the Block.

■ The Block has ownership of the __block variable.

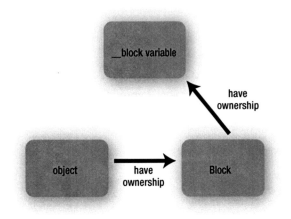

Figure 5–13. *Avoiding circular reference*

Compare the two approaches: one with __block variable and the other with the __weak or __unsafe_unretained ownership qualifier.

The advantages of the approach with __block variable are:

- You can control the lifetime of the object by controlling __block variable.

- Even for an environment that doesn't support the __weak ownership qualifier, you don't need to use the __unsafe_unretained ownership qualifier and you don't need to be afraid of a dangling pointer.

This means that while the Block is executed, you can control assigning nil or another object to the __block variable dynamically.

In contrast, the disadvantage of the approach with a __block variable is that

- You have to execute the Block to avoid a circular reference.

After the Block literal is executed, if the application doesn't execute the Block, circular reference can't be avoided. If a circular reference occurs because of the Block, you have to decide how to solve it with a __block variable or __weak or __unsafe_unretained ownership qualifier, depending on how the Block is used.

Copy/Release

When ARC is disabled, to copy a Block from the stack to the heap, you always have to do it manually. And, because ARC is disabled, you have to release the Block manually as well. You use an instance method "copy" and "release" as follows.

```
void (^blk_on_heap)(void) = [blk_on_stack copy];

[blk_on_heap release];
```

Also, you can take ownership of a Block, which is already copied to the heap, with the instance method "retain".

```
[blk_on_heap retain];
```

When you call "retain" to a Block on the stack, unfortunately, nothing happens.

```
[blk_on_stack retain];
```

In this source code, the instance method "retain" is called to a Block on the stack, which is assigned to the "blk_on_stack" and nothing really happens. So, to take ownership of a Block, I recommend that you always call instance method "copy".

Also, because Block is a C language extension, you can use Block syntax in C. In this case, you can use "Block_copy" and "Block_release" functions, instead of "copy" and "release" methods in Objective-C. The concept of the reference count and how to use it are just same as the copy and release methods.

```
void (^blk_on_heap)(void) = Block_copy(blk_on_stack);

Block_release(blk_on_heap);
```

The "Block_copy" function works just like _Block_copy, which we've already learned. This function is there for C language and, in fact, the Objective-C runtime library uses it. In the same manner, when a Block on the heap is released, the "Block_release" function is called from the Objective-C runtime library.

By the way, without ARC, a __block specifier can be used to avoid a circular reference, which a Block causes. Because, as its specification says, when a Block is copied from the stack to the heap, and uses an id or object type automatic variable, if the variable is without a __block specifier, the object is retained; on the contrary, with a __block specifier, the object isn't retained. For example, regardless of whether ARC is enabled or disabled, the following source code causes circular reference because a Block has ownership of self, and self has ownership of the Block.

```
typedef void (^blk_t)(void);

@interface MyObject : NSObject
{
    blk_t blk_;
}
@end

@implementation MyObject
- (id)init
{
    self = [super init];
    blk_ = ^{NSLog(@"self = %@", self);};
    return self;
}

- (void)dealloc
{
    NSLog(@"dealloc");
}
@end
```

```
int main()
{
    id o = [[MyObject alloc] init];
    NSLog(@"%@", o);
    return 0;
}
```

For an ARC-disabled environment, you can use a __block variable to solve the problem.

```
- (id)init {
    self = [super init];
    __block id tmp = self;
    blk_ = ^{NSLog(@"self = %@", tmp);};
    return self;
}
```

It works just like the __unsafe_unretained ownership qualifier in an ARC-enabled environment. The purpose of __block specifier is much different depending on ARC being enabled or disabled. So, you have to take care that the source code is for an ARC-enabled environment or not.

Summary

In this chapter, we had deep discussions of Blocks, seeing how Blocks are compiled using clang. Especially, we learned:

- How automatic variables are captured

- How __block variables are achieved

- How a circular reference problem occurs due to captured objects and how to solve it

Blocks are very powerful if you use them with Grand Central Dispatch which we cover in the next chapters.

Chapter 6

Grand Central Dispatch

In the final three chapters, we discuss Grand Central Dispatch (GCD). This new feature is introduced for OS X Snow Leopard and iOS 4 or later to help multithreaded programming. I explain it with the implementation to see how multithreaded programming would be changed.

In this chapter, we first take a glance at an example that uses GCD. We then review what multithreading is now with the benefit of GCD and how traditional multithreading programming was used prior to GCD.

Grand Central Dispatch Overview

Let's see what Apple says about Grand Central Dispatch:

> *One of the technologies for starting tasks asynchronously is Grand Central Dispatch (GCD). This technology takes the thread management code you would normally write in your own applications and moves that code down to the system level. All you have to do is define the tasks you want to execute and add them to an appropriate dispatch queue. GCD takes care of creating the needed threads and of scheduling your tasks to run on those threads. Because the thread management is now part of the system, GCD provides a holistic approach to task management and execution, providing better efficiency than traditional threads.*

It seems that Grand Central Dispatch is an innovative technology to make multithreaded source code unbelievably elegant. Let's see if that is true and how it is achieved with an example. Although it is a bit abstract, it shows the power of GCD.

```
dispatch_async(queue_for_background_threads, ^{
    /*
     * Here, processing a time-consuming task
     * such as AR image processing, database accessing, etc.
```

```
   */

  /*
   * The task is completed. Then, use the result on the main thread as follows.
   */

  dispatch_async(dispatch_get_main_queue(), ^{

      /*
       * Here, tasks that work only on the main, such as
       * updating user inteface, etc.
       */
  });
});
```

This example is for processing a time-consuming task on a background thread and using the result on the main thread.

```
dispatch_async(queue_for_background_threads, ^{
```

This single line makes the task work on a background thread.

```
dispatch_async(dispatch_get_main_queue(), ^{
```

This single line also makes a task work on the main thread. As you can see, carets "^" and Blocks are used to make the source code simple as we've learned in the previous chapters. It seems that what Apple says is true. Next, let's briefly review what multithreaded source code looks like. Before GCD was introduced, Cocoa Framework had mechanisms to support multithreaded programming, such as NSObject class instance methods, performSelectorInBackground:withObject, performSelectorOnMainThread, and so on.

Let's see how the previous example could be written with the performSelector method family.

```
 /*
  * Start a task on a background thread
  * by NSObject performSelectorInBackground:withObject: method.
  */
- (void) launchThreadByNSObject_performSelectorInBackground_withObject
{
    [self performSelectorInBackground:@selector(doWork) withObject:nil];
}

 /*
  * A method to be executed on a background thread.
  */
- (void) doWork
{
    NSAutoreleasePool *pool = [[NSAutoreleasePool alloc] init];

    /*
     * Here, processing a time-consuming task,
     * such as AR image processing,
     * database accessing, etc.
     */
```

```
    /*
     * The task is completed. Next, use the result on the main thread as follows.
     */

    [self performSelectorOnMainThread:@selector(doneWork)
        withObject:nil waitUntilDone:NO];
    [pool drain];
}

 /*
  * A method to be executed on the main thread.
  */
- (void) doneWork
{
    /*
     * A task that can work only on the main thread should be here,
     * such as updating user interface, etc.
     */
}
```

Although the source code for multithreaded programming using the performSelector method family is easier than a source code using the NSThread class, the source code with GCD is obviously the simplest.

Multithreaded programming with GCD is more elegant than with the performSelector method family. You don't need to use messy APIs of the NSThread class or the performSelector method family. Also, it works more effectively. It's just all good!

> **NOTE:** When you'd like to release the NSAutorelease Pool object, calling "drain" instead of "release" is recommended. By "drain" the pool is released immediately even in an environment with garbage collection enabled. If garbage collection is not used, there is no problem in simply using "release."

Multithreaded Programming

As explained, GCD is a technology to make multithreading programming elegant. Before learning GCD itself, we review traditional multithreaded programming.

Also, to take proper advantage of multithreading, you should have a basic idea of how your application is executed on a Mac or iPhone. Let's take a look at them first.

Please glance at some very simple Objective-C source code.

```
int main()
{
    id o = [[MyObject alloc] init];

    [o execBlock];

    return 0;
}
```

There are some method calls but, basically, it is just executed top to bottom as shown in Figure 6–1.

Program

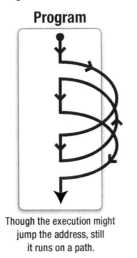

Though the execution might
jump the address, still
it runs on a path.

Figure 6–1. *A CPU executes CPU bytecodes*

Do you know how the source code works on the Mac or iPhone? To execute it on a computer, the compiler converts it to CPU bytecodes as follows. You don't need to understand all the meanings, but we can know that the simple source code is converted to the long sequence of commands.

```
000001ac:      b590 push {r4, r7, lr}
000001ae: f240019c movw r1, :lower16:0x260-0x1c0+0xfffffffc
000001b2:      af01 add  r7, sp, #4
000001b4: f2c00100 movt r1, :upper16:0x260-0x1c0+0xfffffffc
000001b8: f24010be movw r0, :lower16:0x384-0x1c2+0xfffffffc
000001bc: f2c00000 movt r0, :upper16:0x384-0x1c2+0xfffffffc
000001c0:      4479 add  r1, pc
000001c2:      4478 add  r0, pc
000001c4:      6809 ldr  r1, [r1, #0]
000001c6:      6800 ldr  r0, [r0, #0]
000001c8: f7ffef1a blx  _objc_msgSend
000001cc: f2400180 movw r1, :lower16:0x258-0x1d4+0xfffffffc
000001d0: f2c00100 movt r1, :upper16:0x258-0x1d4+0xfffffffc
000001d4:      4479 add  r1, pc
000001d6:      6809 ldr  r1, [r1, #0]
000001d8: f7ffef12 blx  _objc_msgSend
000001dc:      4604 mov  r4, r0
000001de: f240007a movw r0, :lower16:0x264-0x1e6+0xfffffffc
000001e2: f2c00000 movt r0, :upper16:0x264-0x1e6+0xfffffffc
000001e6:      4478 add  r0, pc
000001e8:      6801 ldr  r1, [r0, #0]
000001ea:      4620 mov  r0, r4
000001ec: f7ffef08 blx  _objc_msgSend
000001f0:      4620 mov  r0, r4
000001f2: f7ffef06 blx  _objc_release
000001f6:      2000 movs r0, #0
000001f8:      bd90 pop  {r4, r7, pc}
```

How a CPU Executes an Application

As we saw, the source code is converted to CPU bytecodes. Applications package such bytecode inside in addition to data to be installed on a Mac or iPhone. When a user starts the application on operating systems such as OSX for Mac or iOS for iPhone, the bytecodes are allocated on the memory, and, the CPU executes the bytecodes one by one, starting with an address that is specified in the application.

In the example, an instruction "push" on the initial address "1ac" is executed first. Then, it goes to the next address. The next instruction "movw" on the address "1ae" is executed, then the instruction on "1b2", and so on.

The executing address can jump to a distant address by control statements such as "if", "for", or function calls in Objective-C. One CPU can still execute one instruction at the same moment. The execution never splits to run two instructions concurrently. Sometimes, an analogy of a path is used to explain the execution on the CPU.

A thread is equivalent to a path of the CPU execution. These days, some CPUs have 64 CPU cores; others work as two virtual CPUs. It is very common for one computer to have multiple CPU cores. But one CPU core still runs only one path. Multithread means that an application has many paths. The multithreaded applications can execute multiple paths concurrently as shown in Figure 6–2.

Program

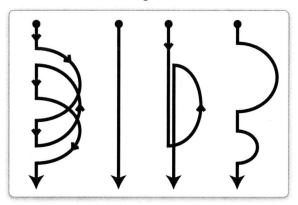

Figure 6–2. *CPU executes bytecodes on multithread*

There are many CPU-related technologies and they evolve rapidly, still one CPU core can execute just one CPU bytecode. How can multithreaded applications execute bytecodes on multiple paths?

The XNU kernel that is a core part of OS X and iOS switches between the paths at regular time intervals and when it get an OS event, such as system calls, an executing state for a path, including CPU registers, is stored in one of the memory blocks assigned to each path. And the other executing state is copied back from a memory block to the

CPU registers, and so on; that is, the CPU continues executing on this path. This mechanism is called a "context switch." A multithreaded program repeats context switches over and over. Because of that, one CPU can virtually execute multiple threads. When there are multiple CPU cores, each core can run a thread in parallel. In this case, the number of threads equals the number of CPU cores that can really run in parallel. Programming techniques for multithreading are called "multithreaded programming."

Advantages and Disadvantages of Multithreaded Programming

Multithreaded programming causes many problems. For example, when multiple threads compete to update the same resource, it causes inconsistent data (called a *race condition*). When multiple threads await an event at the same time (*deadlock*), these threads stack. When too many threads are used, the application memory becomes short, and so on (Figure 6–3).

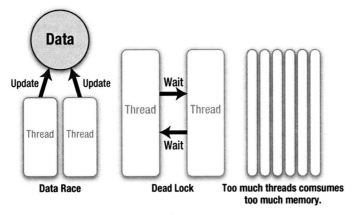

Figure 6–3. *Problems of multi threaded programming*

Of course there are many methods to avoid these problems, but the source code rapidly becomes too complex. With all of these problems, why is multithreaded programming still used?

The reason is to make the application highly responsive. In an application, a thread is started just after the application is launched. The thread draws user interfaces, handles events from a touch panel, and so on. This thread is called the *main thread*. If the main thread executes a time-consuming task, such as image processing for AR or database access, the task blocks all the other tasks on the main thread. On OSX and iOS, the main loop, called RunLoop on the main thread, should not be blocked because only the main thread can update user interfaces. When it is blocked, user interfaces aren't updated and the same still image is displayed for quite a long time. To avoid such a situation, time-consuming tasks should be executed on the other threads as shown in Figure 6–4.

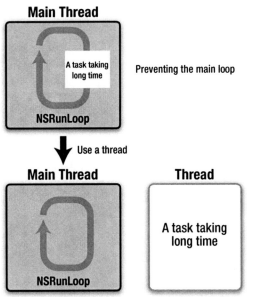

Figure 6–4. *Multithreaded programming advantages*

In a multithreaded application, the user interface can still be responsive while the time-consuming task is running. GCD also makes multithreaded programming very elegant. In the next chapter, we show how to use GCD API.

Summary

In this chapter, we learned what multithreaded programming is and its advantages and disadvantages. In the next chapter, we learn the basic mechanism of GCD and GCD APIs. We also show how GCD is better than traditional multithreaded programming.

Chapter 7

GCD Basics

In this chapter, we show how to use GCD. At first, we start with a dispatch queue that is a core concept of GCD and show how to add tasks to the queues. After that, we design an API to control queues and tasks. Finally, we also show how to dispatch I/0 to control files using GCD.

Dispatch Queues

A dispatch queue is, as its name suggests, a queue to store tasks to be executed. Application programmers can write tasks as Block literals and add them to a dispatch queue by a dispatch_async function, and the like. Then the dispatch queue executes the tasks in the added order, first-in-first-out (FIFO), as shown in Figure 7–1.

Dispatch Queue

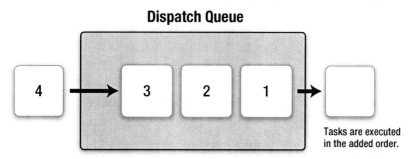

Tasks are executed
in the added order.

Figure 7–1. *Execution on a dispatch queue*

As shown in Figure 7–2, there are two kinds of dispatch queues. One is a serial dispatch queue, which waits until the current running task finishes before starting another task. The other is a concurrent dispatch queue, which doesn't wait.

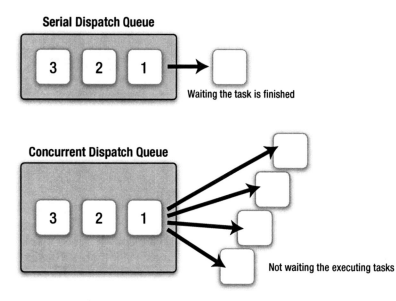

Figure 7–2. *Serial Dispatch Queue and Concurrent Dispatch Queue*

Two Types of Dispatch Queue

Let's compare the two types of dispatch queues. The following source code adds tasks to the dispatch queue using the dispatch_async function.

```
dispatch_async(queue, blk0);
dispatch_async(queue, blk1);
dispatch_async(queue, blk2);
dispatch_async(queue, blk3);
dispatch_async(queue, blk4);
dispatch_async(queue, blk5);
dispatch_async(queue, blk6);
dispatch_async(queue, blk7);
```

Let's take a look at how it works when the variable "queue" is a serial dispatch queue that waits until the current running task is finished.

Serial Dispatch Queue

Firstly, blk0 is started. Next, blk1 is started after blk0 is finished. Then blk2 is started when the blk1 is finished, and so on. Only one task runs at a time, which means that the result is always the same. The blocks are executed as

```
blk0
blk1
blk2
blk3
blk4
blk5
blk6
blk7
```

Next, let's see how it works when the variable "queue" is a concurrent dispatch queue that doesn't wait for the running tasks to complete.

Concurrent Dispatch Queue

Firstly, blk0 is started, and whether it finishes or not, blk1 is started, then regardless of whether blk1 is finished, blk2 is started, and so on. It doesn't wait until the tasks are finished and multiple tasks run concurrently, but please note that the number of tasks running concurrently depends on the status of the current system; that is, iOS or OS X decides the number based on the current system status, such as how many tasks are in the dispatch queue, the number of CPU cores, or the CPU usage level. The multiple tasks can run concurrently by using multiple threads under the hood as shown in Figure 7–3.

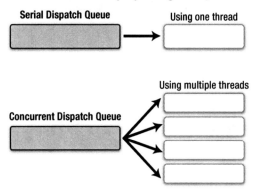

Figure 7–3. *Relationship of Serial Dispatch Queue, Concurrent Dispatch Queue, and threads*

The XNU kernel, which is a core part of iOS and OS X, decides the number of threads. It also creates threads to execute the tasks. When a task is finished and the number of running tasks is decreased, the XNU kernel terminates an unneeded thread. Just by using a concurrent dispatch queue, the XNU kernel manages multiple threads perfectly to run tasks concurrently. For instance, the source code is executed on multiple threads as in shown in Table 7–1.

Table 7–1. *The example result with a concurrent dispatch queue*

Thread0	Thread1	Thread2	Thread3
blk0	blk1	blk2	blk3
blk4	blk6	blk5	
blk7			

Let's assume that four threads are prepared for the concurrent dispatch queue. At first, blk0 is started on thread0. Next, blk1 is started on thread1, blk2 on thread2, and blk3 on thread3. Then, blk4 is started on thread0 because blk0 is finished. Next, blk5 is started on thread2 because blk1 is still running on thread1 and blk2 is finished on thread2.

In that manner, when a concurrent dispatch queue is used, the execution order depends on the tasks themselves, the system status, and so on. The order of the tasks isn't constant as with a serial dispatch queue. You should use the serial dispatch queue when the order is important or the tasks shouldn't be running concurrently.

Now we know that there are two types of dispatch queues, a serial dispatch queue and a concurrent dispatch queue. How can we obtain these queues? You're about to find out.

Obtaining Dispatch Queues

There are two ways to do that, with `dispatch_queue_create` and `main dispatch queue / global dispatch queue`. The following sections discuss both of these.

dispatch_queue_create

The dispatch_queue_create is a function for creating a dispatch queue. You can obtain a new dispatch queue with this function. Next, the source code shows how to create a serial dispatch queue. You can also create a concurrent dispatch queue as well. I explain it later in this section.

```
dispatch_queue_t mySerialDispatchQueue =
dispatch_queue_create("com.example.gcd.MySerialDispatchQueue", NULL);
```

When you create a serial dispatch queue, it is independent of other serial queues, even though they all only execute one task at a time. For example, four separate serial queues with one task each, all started at the same time, would start executing simultaneously as shown in Figure 7–4.

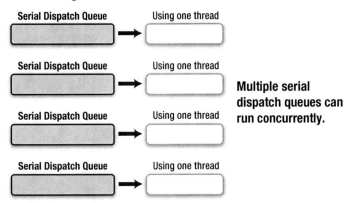

Figure 7–4. *Multiple Serial Dispatch Queues*

We must know one thing related to that. When a serial dispatch queue is created and a task is added, the system creates one thread for each serial dispatch queue. If 2,000 serial dispatch queues are created, 2,000 threads are created. As I explained, too many threads consume too much memory and too many context switches cause the system to slow down as shown in Figure 7–5.

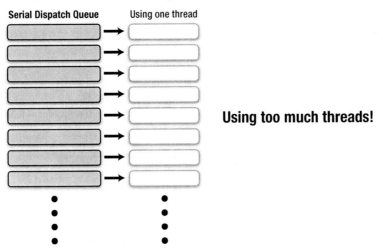

Figure 7–5. *Problem of multiple Serial Dispatch Queues*

That is why you should use a serial dispatch queue only to avoid inconsistent data (race condition) that occurs because multiple threads update the same data, which I explained as one of the problems of multithreaded programming (Figure7–6).

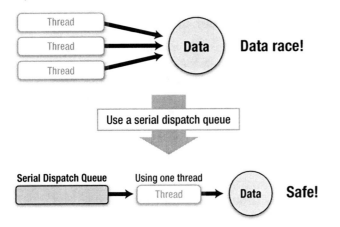

Figure 7–6. *Situation where a Serial Dispatch Queue should be used*

The number of serial dispatch queues should be the same amount that you need. For example, when you update a database, you should create one serial dispatch queue for each table. When you update a file, you should create a serial dispatch queue for the file or for each separated file block. Don't create too many serial dispatch queues even if you think that you can create more threads than using a concurrent dispatch queue. If the tasks don't cause problems such as inconsistent data and you want to execute them concurrently, you should use a concurrent dispatch queue. Even if a concurrent dispatch queue is created again and again, there is no problem because the queues just use threads that are managed efficiently by the XNU kernel.

Let's get back to the dispatch_queue_create function. The first argument for the dispatch_queue_create function is the name of a serial dispatch queue. As in the source code, reverse-order FQDN is recommended for it. It is displayed as the name of the dispatch queue when you are debugging with Xcode or Instruments. The CrashLog that is generated when the application crashes includes that as well. So, it should be something understandable for you, as the application programmer, and not embarrassing for users. If you feel bothered, you can just use NULL. You'll regret it when you debug the application, though.

For the second argument, you should pass NULL to create a serial dispatch queue. To create a concurrent dispatch queue, pass DISPATCH_QUEUE_CONCURRENT as follows.

```
dispatch_queue_t myConcurrentDispatchQueue = dispatch_queue_create(
    "com.example.gcd.MyConcurrentDispatchQueue", DISPATCH_QUEUE_CONCURRENT);
```

The return type of the dispatch_queue_create function is dispatch_queue_t, which is a variable type for dispatch queues. In all the previous examples, a variable "queue" is a dispatch_queue_t type.

```
dispatch_queue_t myConcurrentDispatchQueue = dispatch_queue_create(
    "com.example.gcd.MyConcurrentDispatchQueue", DISPATCH_QUEUE_CONCURRENT);

dispatch_async(myConcurrentDispatchQueue,
    ^{NSLog(@"block on myConcurrentDispatchQueue");});
```

In this source code, the Block runs in the concurrent dispatch queue.

Unfortunately, although the compiler has a great automatic memory management mechanism, ARC, application programmers have to release created dispatch queues manually because a dispatch queue, unlike a Block, isn't treated as an Objective-C object. When you no longer need it, you have to call the dispatch_release function to release the dispatch queue that is created by dispatch_queue_create function.

```
dispatch_release(mySerialDispatchQueue);
```

As the name contains "release", the "dispatch_retain" function is there as well.

```
dispatch_retain(myConcurrentDispatchQueue);
```

This means that dispatch queues have to be managed by the dispatch_retain and dispatch_release functions with the reference counting technique as for objects in Objective-C. In the previous source code, the concurrent dispatch queue that is created by the dispatch_queue_create function and is assigned to the variable "myConcurrentDispatchQueue" has to be released.

```
dispatch_queue_t myConcurrentDispatchQueue = dispatch_queue_create(
    "com.example.gcd.MyConcurrentDispatchQueue", DISPATCH_QUEUE_CONCURRENT);

dispatch_async(myConcurrentDispatchQueue,
    ^{NSLog(@"block on myConcurrentDispatchQueue");});

dispatch_release(myConcurrentDispatchQueue);
```

A concurrent dispatch queue executes tasks using multiple threads. In this example, the concurrent dispatch queue is released by the dispatch_release function just after a Block is added by the dispatch_async function. Does it work safely?

It works just fine. When a Block is added to a dispatch queue by a dispatch_async function, say, the Block has ownership of the dispatch queue by the dispatch_retain function. It is the same for both a serial and a concurrent dispatch queue. Then, when it finishes the execution of the Block, the Block releases the dispatch queue by the dispatch_release function.

Even if a dispatch queue is released just after a Block is added to the dispatch queue by the dispatch_async function, the dispatch queue still isn't disposed of and the Block can be executed. After the Block is finished, the Block releases the dispatch queue and it is discarded. The dispatch_retain and dispatch_release functions are not only for dispatch queues. From now on, we will see many GCD APIs that contain "create" in their names. When you get something from these APIs, you have to release them with the dispatch_release function when you don't need them anymore. When you get them via some other method, you have to take ownership by the dispatch_retain function and you have to release them by the dispatch_release function.

Main Dispatch Queue/Global Dispatch Queue

The other way to obtain a dispatch queue is to get a dispatch queue that the system has already provided. Actually, the system has dispatch queues that you don't create: the main dispatch and global dispatch queues.

The main dispatch queue is, as "main" is in its name, a queue to execute tasks on the main thread. As there exists only one main thread, the main dispatch queue is a serial dispatch queue. Tasks in the main dispatch queue are executed in RunLoop on the main thread as shown in Figure 7–7. Because they are executed on the main thread, you should use it for tasks that must be done on the main thread such as updating the user interface, and the like. It is just like the performSelectorOnMainThread instance method of the NSObject class.

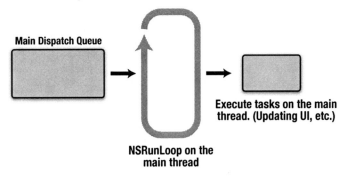

Figure 7–7. *Main Dispatch Queue*

The other queues that the system provides are called global dispatch queues. They are concurrent dispatch queues that are usable anywhere in the application. If you don't have any specific reason, as explained later, you don't need to create a concurrent dispatch queue by the dispatch_queue_create function in most cases. You can just obtain a global dispatch queue and use it. There are four global dispatch queues and they each have a different priority: high, default, low, and background. The XNU kernel manages threads for the global dispatch queues and the threads have priorities corresponding to each priority of the global dispatch queues. When you add tasks to a global dispatch queue, you should choose a global dispatch queue having the appropriate priority. The XNU kernel doesn't assure the realtimeness for threads. So, the priorities can be used just as a guide. For example, you should use a background priority when you don't much care if a task is executed. Let's see what types of dispatch queues are provided in the system in Table 7–2.

Table 7–2. *Types of dispatch queues*

Name	Type	Description
Main dispatch queue	Serial dispatch queue	Executed on the main thread
Global dispatch queue (High priority)	Concurrent dispatch queue	Priority: High (Utmost priority)
Global dispatch queue (Default priority)	Concurrent dispatch queue	Priority: Normal
Global dispatch queue (Low priority)	Concurrent dispatch queue	Priority: Low
Global dispatch queue (Background priority)	Concurrent dispatch queue	Priority: Background

Each dispatch queue can be obtained as shown in Listing 7–1.

Listing 7–1. *Obtaining dispatch queues*

```
/*
 * How to get the main dispatch queue
 */
dispatch_queue_t mainDispatchQueue = dispatch_get_main_queue();

/*
 * How to get a global dispatch queue of high priority
 */
dispatch_queue_t globalDispatchQueueHigh =
        dispatch_get_global_queue(DISPATCH_QUEUE_PRIORITY_HIGH, 0);

/*
 * How to get a global dispatch queue of default priority
 */
dispatch_queue_t globalDispatchQueueDefault =
        dispatch_get_global_queue(DISPATCH_QUEUE_PRIORITY_DEFAULT, 0);
```

```
/*
 * How to get a global dispatch queue of low priority
 */
dispatch_queue_t globalDispatchQueueLow =
        dispatch_get_global_queue(DISPATCH_QUEUE_PRIORITY_LOW, 0);

/*
 * How to get a global dispatch queue of background priority
 */
dispatch_queue_t globalDispatchQueueBackground =
        dispatch_get_global_queue(DISPATCH_QUEUE_PRIORITY_BACKGROUND, 0);
```

By the way, if you call the dispatch_retain or dispatch_release function on the main dispatch queue or on a global dispatch queue, nothing happens. No problem. That is why it is easier to obtain and use a global dispatch queue than to create, use, and release a concurrent dispatch queue yourself. Of course, depending on your source code, if it is easier for the dispatch queue to be treated as it is created by the dispatch_queue_create function, you can follow the concept of reference counting rules and call the dispatch_retain or dispatch_release function even for the main dispatch queue or a global dispatch queue.

At the end of this section, there is an example of how to use the main dispatch queue and global dispatch queues as shown in Listing 7–2.

Listing 7–2. *Executing tasks*

```
/*
 * Execute a Block on a global dispatch queue of default priority.
 */
dispatch_async(dispatch_get_global_queue(DISPATCH_QUEUE_PRIORITY_DEFAULT, 0), ^{

    /*
     * some tasks here to be executed concurrently
     */

    /*
     * Then, execute a Block on the main dispatch queue
     */

    dispatch_async(dispatch_get_main_queue(), ^{

        /*
         * Here, some tasks that can work only on the main thread.
         */
    });

});
```

We've learned the basics of GCD for making tasks run in parallel. In the following section, I explain APIs to control the queues to make them more useful.

Controlling Dispatch Queues

GCD also provides many useful APIs to control the tasks in the dispatch queues. Let's see the APIs one by one to explore how GCD is so powerful.

dispatch_set_target_queue

The dispatch_set_target_queue function is for setting a "target" queue. This is mainly used to set the priority to a newly created queue. For both serial and concurrent dispatch queues, when a dispatch queue is created by the dispatch_queue_create function, the priority of the thread is the same as that of a global dispatch queue of default priority. To modify the priority of a dispatch queue after it is created, you can use this function to modify it. The following source code shows how to get a serial dispatch queue to be executed on the background priority.

```
dispatch_queue_t mySerialDispatchQueue =
    dispatch_queue_create("com.example.gcd.MySerialDispatchQueue", NULL);

dispatch_queue_t globalDispatchQueueBackground =
    dispatch_get_global_queue(DISPATCH_QUEUE_PRIORITY_BACKGROUND, 0);

dispatch_set_target_queue(mySerialDispatchQueue, globalDispatchQueueBackground);
```

In the source code, the dispatch queue is passed as the first argument for the dispatch_set_target_queue function to change the priority of the dispatch queue. As the second argument, a global dispatch queue is passed as its target. The mechanism is explained later, though, The result is that the priority of the dispatch queue is changed to the same priority as that of the target queue. The behavior is undefined when you pass the main or the global dispatch queues that are provided by the system as the first argument. So you shouldn't do that. Using the dispatch_set_target_queue function, you can not only change the priority, but you can also create a hierarchy of dispatch queues as shown in Figure 7–8. When a serial dispatch queue is set as the target for multiple serial dispatch queues that will be executed concurrently for the dispatch_set_target_queue function, only one queue is executed on the target serial dispatch queue at a time.

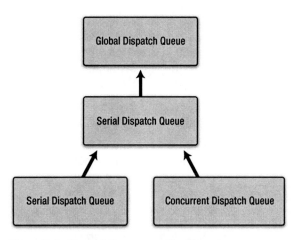

Figure 7–8. *Dispatch Queue execution hierarchy*

By doing that, you can prevent the tasks executing concurrently if you have tasks that shouldn't be executed concurrently and they must be added to different serial dispatch queues. Actually, I have no idea of such a situation, though.

dispatch_after

dispatch _after is for setting the timing to start tasks in the queue. Sometimes you may want to execute a task three seconds later, for instance. When you want to execute a task after some specified time has passed, you can use the dispatch_after function. For example, the following source code adds the specified Block to the main dispatch queue after three seconds.

```
dispatch_time_t time = dispatch_time(DISPATCH_TIME_NOW, 3ull * NSEC_PER_SEC);

dispatch_after(time, dispatch_get_main_queue(), ^{

        NSLog(@"waited at least three seconds.");

});
```

In the source code, "ull" is a C language literal specifying a type. "ull" is for "unsigned long long" type. Please note that the dispatch_after function doesn't execute the task after the specified time. After the time, it adds the task to the dispatch queue, meaning that this source code works the same as if you added the Block to the main dispatch queue by the dispatch_async function three seconds later. The main dispatch queue is executed in RunLoop on the main thread. So, for example, if the RunLoop is executed at a 1/60 second interval, the Block will be executed between after three seconds and after three + 1/60 seconds. If many tasks are added in the main dispatch queue, or if the main thread is delayed, it could get behind. Therefore, it is problematic to use it as an accurate timer, but if you just want to delay a task roughly, this function is very useful. The second argument specifies a dispatch queue to add a task, and the third argument is a Block to be executed. The first argument is a value of dispatch_time_t type to specify the time. This value is created by the dispatch_time or dispatch_walltime function. The dispatch_time function creates a time value, the nanoseconds (the second argument) that have elapsed after a time (the first argument) in dispatch_time_t type. As in the example, DISPATCH_TIME_NOW is mostly used for the first argument to specify the current time. In the following source code, you can get a time in a dispatch_time_t type variable to specify one second from now.

```
dispatch_time_t time = dispatch_time(DISPATCH_TIME_NOW, 1ull * NSEC_PER_SEC);
```

The product of the number and NSEC_PER_SEC makes a time in units of nanoseconds. With NSEC_PER_MSEC, you can make millisecond unit values. The next source code shows how to get a time of 150 milliseconds from now.

```
dispatch_time_t time = dispatch_time(DISPATCH_TIME_NOW, 150ull * NSEC_PER_MSEC);
```

The dispatch_walltime function creates a time in a dispatch_time_t type from a time of struct "timespec" that is used in POSIX. The dispatch_time function is used mainly to create a relative time. In contrast, the dispatch_walltime function is used to create an absolute time. For example, you can use dispatch_walltime to get an absolute time such as 11:11:11 on November 11, 2011 for the dispatch_after function. You can create an alarm clock with that, but it is low precision. A time of timespec struct type is created easily from the NSDate class object as shown in Listing 7–3.

Listing 7–3. *dispatch_time_t from NSDate*

```
dispatch_time_t getDispatchTimeByDate(NSDate *date)
{
    NSTimeInterval interval;
    double second, subsecond;
    struct timespec time;
    dispatch_time_t milestone;

    interval = [date timeIntervalSince1970];
    subsecond = modf(interval, &second);
    time.tv_sec = second;
    time.tv_nsec = subsecond * NSEC_PER_SEC;
    milestone = dispatch_walltime(&time, 0);

    return milestone;
}
```

In the source code, a value of dispatch_time_t type is created from the NSDate class object and it is passed to the dispatch_after function.

Dispatch Group

Dispatch group is used to make a group of queues. You may want to start a task to finalize something after all the tasks in the dispatch queues are finished. When all the tasks are in one serial dispatch queue, you can just add a finalizing task to the end of the queue. It seems complex when you use a concurrent dispatch queue or multiple dispatch queues. In these cases, you can use a dispatch group. The following source code is to add three Blocks to a global dispatch queue and when all the Blocks are finished, a Block for finalization will be executed on the main dispatch queue.

```
dispatch_queue_t queue =
    dispatch_get_global_queue(DISPATCH_QUEUE_PRIORITY_DEFAULT, 0);
dispatch_group_t group = dispatch_group_create();

dispatch_group_async(group, queue, ^{NSLog(@"blk0");});
dispatch_group_async(group, queue, ^{NSLog(@"blk1");});
dispatch_group_async(group, queue, ^{NSLog(@"blk2");});

dispatch_group_notify(group,
    dispatch_get_main_queue(), ^{NSLog(@"done");});
dispatch_release(group);
```

The result will be like:

```
blk1
blk2
blk0
done
```

The execution order of the tasks is not constant because they are in a global dispatch queue that is a concurrent dispatch queue; that is, the tasks are executed on multiple threads concurrently. The execution timing is not constant. Still, "done" must be displayed at the end every time. A dispatch group can monitor tasks to be finished no matter in which type of dispatch queues they are. When it detects that all the tasks are finished, the finalizing task is added to the dispatch queue. This is how the dispatch group is used. At first, a dispatch group that is of type dispatch_group_t is created by the dispatch_group_create function. As the function name contains "create", the dispatch group has to be released when you don't need it anymore. You should use the dispatch_release function as you use it for a dispatch queue. The dispatch_group_async function adds a Block to the specified dispatch queue as does the dispatch_async function. The difference from the dispatch_async function is that a created dispatch group is passed to its first argument. When the dispatch_group_async function is called, the specified Block is associated with the dispatch group. When a Block is associated with a dispatch group, the Block has ownership of the dispatch group by the dispatch_retain function as if a Block were added to the dispatch queue. When the Block is finished, the Block releases the dispatch group by the dispatch_release function. When you don't need the dispatch group anymore, you should just call dispatch_release to release the dispatch group. You don't need to care how the Blocks that are associated with the dispatch group are executed.

As in the example, the dispatch_group_notify function specifies a Block to be added to a dispatch queue. The Block will be executed when all the tasks in the dispatch group are finished. The first argument is a dispatch group to be monitored. When all the tasks associated with the group are finished, the Block (the third argument) will be added to the dispatch queue (the second argument). Regardless of the type of dispatch queue passed for the dispatch_group_notify function, when the Block is added, all the tasks associated with the dispatch group must be finished.

In addition, you can simply wait to finish all the tasks with a dispatch group. You can use the dispatch_group_wait function as shown in Listing 7–4.

Listing 7–4. *dispatch_group_wait*

```
dispatch_queue_t queue =
    dispatch_get_global_queue(DISPATCH_QUEUE_PRIORITY_DEFAULT, 0);
dispatch_group_t group = dispatch_group_create();

dispatch_group_async(group, queue, ^{NSLog(@"blk0");});
dispatch_group_async(group, queue, ^{NSLog(@"blk1");});
dispatch_group_async(group, queue, ^{NSLog(@"blk2");});

dispatch_group_wait(group, DISPATCH_TIME_FOREVER);
dispatch_release(group);
```

The second argument for the dispatch_group_wait function is a timeout to specify how long it waits. The variable is dispatch_time_t type. This example uses DISPATCH_TIME_FOREVER to wait forever. It waits forever until all the tasks associated with the dispatch group are finished. You can't cancel it in the middle.

As we've learned with the dispatch_after function, you can wait one second in the following source code.

```
dispatch_time_t time = dispatch_time(DISPATCH_TIME_NOW, 1ull * NSEC_PER_SEC);

long result = dispatch_group_wait(group, time);

if (result == 0) {

    /*
     * All the tasks that are associated with the dispatch group are finished
     */

} else {

    /*
     * some tasks that are associated with the dispatch group are still running.
     */
}
```

When the dispatch_group_wait function didn't return zero, some tasks that are associated with the dispatch group were still running even after the specified time had passed. When it returned zero, all the tasks were finished. The dispatch_group_wait function returns zero if DISPATCH_TIME_FOREVER is used because all the tasks must be finished.

By the way, what does "wait" mean? It means that when the dispatch_group_wait function is called, it doesn't return from the function. The current thread that is executing the dispatch_group_wait function stops. While the time that is specified to the dispatch_group_wait function passes, or until all the tasks that are associated with the dispatch group are finished, the thread that is executing the dispatch_group_wait function stops.

When DISPATCH_TIME_NOW is used, you can check if the tasks that are associated with the dispatch group are finished.

```
long result = dispatch_group_wait(group, DISPATCH_TIME_NOW);
```

For example, you can check if the tasks are finished in each loop of the RunLoop on the main thread without any delay. Although it is possible, I recommend using dispatch_group_notify to add some finalizing task to the main dispatch queue instead. Your source code becomes elegant. Still there are many useful functions in GCD. I explain them in the following sections. Let's start with dispatch_barrier_async.

dispatch_barrier_async

The dispatch_barrier_async is a function for waiting for other tasks in a queue. As explained, when you access a database or a file, you can use serial dispatch queues to avoid inconsistent data. Actually, updating data shouldn't be executed at the same time as other updating tasks or reading tasks. Reading data might be able to run concurrently with the other reading tasks, meaning to access the data effectively, the reading tasks should be added to concurrent dispatch queues and only the updating tasks have to be in a serial dispatch queue while no updating task is running. You have to make sure that the reading tasks don't start until the updating tasks are finished. You might be able to implement it with the dispatch group and dispatch_set_target_queue functions, but it seems to be complex. GCD offers a better solution, the dispatch_barrier_async function. This function is used with a concurrent dispatch queue created by the dispatch_queue_create function. The following source code creates a concurrent dispatch queue by the dispatch_queue_create function, and some reading tasks are added by dispatch_async.

```
dispatch_queue_t queue = dispatch_queue_create(
    "com.example.gcd.ForBarrier", DISPATCH_QUEUE_CONCURRENT);

dispatch_async(queue, blk0_for_reading);
dispatch_async(queue, blk1_for_reading);
dispatch_async(queue, blk2_for_reading);
dispatch_async(queue, blk3_for_reading);
dispatch_async(queue, blk4_for_reading);
dispatch_async(queue, blk5_for_reading);
dispatch_async(queue, blk6_for_reading);
dispatch_async(queue, blk7_for_reading);

dispatch_release(queue);
```

Next, for example, think about writing data between the blk3_for_reading and blk4_for_reading, and blk4_for_reading and later tasks should read the updated data.

```
dispatch_async(queue, blk0_for_reading);
dispatch_async(queue, blk1_for_reading);
dispatch_async(queue, blk2_for_reading);
dispatch_async(queue, blk3_for_reading);

 /*
  * Writing data
  *
  * From now on, all the tasks should read the updated data.
  */

dispatch_async(queue, blk4_for_reading);
```

```
dispatch_async(queue, blk5_for_reading);
dispatch_async(queue, blk6_for_reading);
dispatch_async(queue, blk7_for_reading);
```

If we just put the writing task with the dispatch_async function, as in the next source code, even the tasks that are added before the writing task might read the updated data unexpectedly. The application might even crash because of its invalid access. This is the nature of the concurrent dispatch queue. Furthermore if you add writing tasks, it will cause inconsistent data and many more problems will occur.

```
dispatch_async(queue, blk0_for_reading);
dispatch_async(queue, blk1_for_reading);
dispatch_async(queue, blk2_for_reading);
dispatch_async(queue, blk3_for_reading);
dispatch_async(queue, blk_for_writing);
dispatch_async(queue, blk4_for_reading);
dispatch_async(queue, blk5_for_reading);
dispatch_async(queue, blk6_for_reading);
dispatch_async(queue, blk7_for_reading);
```

Here is the dispatch_barrier_async function. Using the dispatch_barrier_async function, you can add a task to a concurrent dispatch queue at the time all the tasks in the queue are finished. When the task added by the dispatch_barrier_async function is finished, the concurrent dispatch queue will be back to normal, which means that it executes the tasks concurrently as usual as shown in Figure 7–9.

```
dispatch_async(queue, blk0_for_reading);
dispatch_async(queue, blk1_for_reading);
dispatch_async(queue, blk2_for_reading);
dispatch_async(queue, blk3_for_reading);
dispatch_barrier_async(queue, blk_for_writing);
dispatch_async(queue, blk4_for_reading);
dispatch_async(queue, blk5_for_reading);
dispatch_async(queue, blk6_for_reading);
dispatch_async(queue, blk7_for_reading);
```

As you see, it is very simple. Just use the dispatch_barrier_async function instead of the dispatch_async function. That's all.

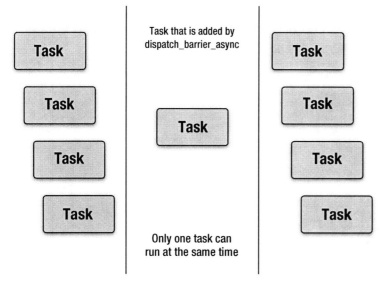

Figure 7–9. *Execution with the dispatch_barrier_async function*

Please use a concurrent dispatch queue and the dispatch_barrier_async function to implement an effective database or file access. Next, let's see a dispatch_sync function that is similar to the dispatch_async function.

dispatch_sync

dispatch_sync is a function similar to dispatch_async, but is waiting for the task to be added. "async" in the name of the dispatch_async function means asynchronous. Thus it adds a Block to a dispatch queue and the task is executed asynchronously. The dispatch_async function doesn't wait for anything as shown in Figure 7–10.

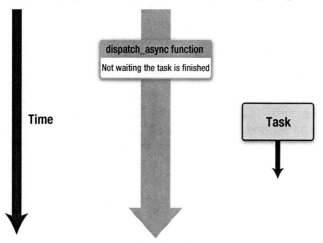

Figure 7–10. *Behavior of dispatch_async function*

There is also a synchronous version, the dispatch_sync function, as well. It adds the Block to the dispatch queue synchronously. The dispatch_sync function waits for the added Block to be finished as shown in Figure 7–11.

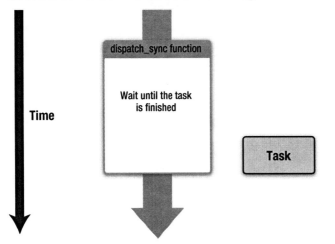

Figure 7–11. *Behavior of dispatch_sync function*

As I explained about the dispatch_group_wait function in the "Dispatch Group" section, "wait" means that the current thread stops. For example, on the main dispatch queue, you might want to use a result of a task that was executed on a global dispatch queue on the other thread. In such a situation, you can use the dispatch_sync function.

```
dispatch_queue_t queue =
    dispatch_get_global_queue(DISPATCH_QUEUE_PRIORITY_DEFAULT, 0);

dispatch_sync(queue, ^{/* a task */});
```

After the dispatch_sync function is called, the function doesn't return until the specified task is finished. It is like a brief version of the dispatch_group_wait function. As you see, the source code is very simple. You can use the dispatch_sync function very easily although it can produce a problem called deadlock. For example, when the following source code is executed on the main thread, it causes a deadlock.

```
dispatch_queue_t queue = dispatch_get_main_queue();
dispatch_sync(queue, ^{NSLog(@"Hello?");});
```

This source code adds a Block to the main dispatch queue; that is, the Block will be executed on the main thread. At the same time, it waits for the block to be finished. Because it is running on the main thread, the Block in the main dispatch queue is never executed. Let's see the other example:

```
dispatch_queue_t queue = dispatch_get_main_queue();
dispatch_async(queue, ^{
    dispatch_sync(queue, ^{NSLog(@"Hello?");});
});
```

The Block that is running on the main dispatch queue is waiting for the other Block to be finished, which will run on the main dispatch queue as well. It causes deadlock.

Of course the same thing happens with a serial dispatch queue.

```
dispatch_queue_t queue =
    dispatch_queue_create("com.example.gcd.MySerialDispatchQueue", NULL);
dispatch_async(queue, ^{
    dispatch_sync(queue, ^{NSLog(@"Hello?");});
});
```

As the name of the dispatch_barrier_async function contains "async", there is a sync version as well, dispatch_barrier_sync. After all the tasks in a dispatch queue are finished, the specified task is added to the dispatch queue as a dispatch_barrier_async function. It waits for the specified task to be finished like the dispatch_sync function. When you use synchronous APIs, such as dispatch_sync, that wait for a task to be finished, you have to ask why you are using the API. You don't want to deadlock the application, do you?

dispatch_apply

dispatch_apply is a function that relates to the dispatch_sync function and dispatch groups. The dispatch_apply function is used to add a Block to a dispatch queue for a number of times, and then it waits until all the tasks are finished.

```
dispatch_queue_t queue =
    dispatch_get_global_queue(DISPATCH_QUEUE_PRIORITY_DEFAULT, 0);
dispatch_apply(10, queue, ^(size_t index) {
    NSLog(@"%zu", index);
});
NSLog(@"done");
```

The result is something like:

```
4
1
0
3
5
2
6
8
9
7
done
```

Because it is executed on the global dispatch queue, the executing timing of each task isn't constant. "done" must always be last because the dispatch_apply function waits for all the tasks to be finished.

The first argument is the number of times, the second is the target dispatch queue, and the third is the task to be added to the queue. In this example, the Block in the third argument takes an argument to distinguish each Block because the Block is added multiple times. For example, when you want to do something for each entry in an NSArray class object, you don't need to write a for-loop. Let's see the following source code. It assumes that an NSArray class object is assigned to a variable "array".

```
dispatch_queue_t queue =
    dispatch_get_global_queue(DISPATCH_QUEUE_PRIORITY_DEFAULT, 0);
dispatch_apply([array count], queue, ^(size_t index) {
    NSLog(@"%zu: %@", index, [array objectAtIndex:index]);
});
```

It is very easy to execute a Block for all the entries in an array on a global dispatch queue. The dispatch_apply function waits for the execution of all the tasks as the dispatch_sync function does. I recommend using the dispatch_apply function with the dispatch_async function to run it asynchronously as shown in Listing 7–5.

Listing 7–5. *dispatch_apply*

```
dispatch_queue_t queue =
    dispatch_get_global_queue(DISPATCH_QUEUE_PRIORITY_DEFAULT, 0);

/*
 * Executing on a global dispatch queue asynchronously
 */

dispatch_async(queue, ^{

    /*
     * On the global dispatch queue, dispatch_apply function waitsfor all the tasks to
be finished.
     */

    dispatch_apply([array count], queue, ^(size_t index) {

        /*
         * do something concurrently with all the objects in the NSArray object
         */

        NSLog(@"%zu: %@", index, [array objectAtIndex:index]);

    });

    /*
     * All the tasks by dispatch_apply function are finished.
     */

    /*
     * Execute on the main dispatch queue asynchronously
     */

    dispatch_async(dispatch_get_main_queue(), ^{

        /*
         * Executed on the main dispatch queue.
         * Something like updating userface, etc.
         */

        NSLog(@"done");

    });
});
```

Next, let's see the dispatch_suspend and dispatch_resume functions that control the execution of the added tasks.

dispatch_suspend/dispatch_resume

These functions suspend or resume the execution of the queue. When you add many tasks to a dispatch queue, sometimes you don't want to execute the tasks until you finish adding all of them. You may want to do that when a Block captures some values that are affected by other tasks. You can suspend a dispatch queue and resume it later if you would like to execute it then. A dispatch queue can be suspended by the dispatch_suspend function:

```
dispatch_suspend(queue);
```

It can be resumed by the dispatch_resume function:

```
dispatch_resume(queue);
```

It doesn't affect any tasks that are already running. It just prevents starting tasks that are in the dispatch queue but not yet begun. After they are resumed, these tasks will be executed.

Dispatch Semaphore

A dispatch semaphore is useful if you need a concurrency control for a small portion of the source code that has smaller granularity than a serial dispatch queue or dispatch_barrier_async function.

As explained, if data are updated concurrently, inconsistent data might occur or the application might crash. You can avoid that by using a serial dispatch queue or the dispatch_barrier_async function. But sometimes concurrency control has to be done in smaller granularity. Let's see an example to show how to add all the data to an NSMutableArray when the order is unimportant, as shown in Listing 7–6.

Listing 7–6. *Adding data to NSMutableArray*

```
dispatch_queue_t queue =
    dispatch_get_global_queue(DISPATCH_QUEUE_PRIORITY_DEFAULT, 0);

NSMutableArray *array = [[NSMutableArray alloc] init];

for (int i = 0; i < 100000; ++i) {
    dispatch_async(queue, ^{

        [array addObject:[NSNumber numberWithInt:i]];

    });
}
```

In this source code, the object of the NSMutableArray class is updated on a global dispatch queue, which means that the object is updated by multiple threads at the same time. Because the NSMutableArray class doesn't support multithreading, when the object is updated from many threads, it will be corrupted. The application probably crashes because of a memory-related problem. This is a race condition. We can use a dispatch semaphore in this case. A dispatch semaphore should be used for smaller granularity though; we use this example to explain how to use a dispatch semaphore. A dispatch semaphore is a semaphore with a counter, which is called a counting semaphore in multithreaded programming. A semaphore is named after a traffic control with flags. A flag is up when you can go, and the flag is down when you can't. A dispatch semaphore has a counter to simulate the flag. When the counter is zero, the execution waits. When the counter is more than zero, it keeps going after it decrements the counter. Let's see how to use a dispatch semaphore. The following source code is creating a dispatch semaphore with the dispatch_semaphore_create function.

```
dispatch_semaphore_t semaphore = dispatch_semaphore_create(1);
```

The argument is an initial value of the counter. In the example, the counter is initialized as one. As its name includes "create", you have to release it with the dispatch_release function as for a dispatch queue or a dispatch group. You can have ownership by calling the dispatch_retain function as well.

```
dispatch_semaphore_wait(semaphore, DISPATCH_TIME_FOREVER);
```

A dispatch_semaphore_wait function waits until the counter of the dispatch semaphore becomes one and more. When the counter is one and more, or the counter becomes one and more while it is waiting, it decreases the counter and returns from the dispatch_semaphore_wait function. The second argument specifies how long it waits in dispatch_time_t type. In this example, it waits forever. The return value of the dispatch_semaphore_wait function is the same as that of the dispatch_group_wait function. You can switch the behavior by the return value as shown in Listing 7–7.

Listing 7–7. *dispatch_semaphore_wait*

```
dispatch_time_t time = dispatch_time(DISPATCH_TIME_NOW, 1ull * NSEC_PER_SEC);

long result = dispatch_semaphore_wait(semaphore, time);

if (result == 0) {

    /*
     * The counter of the dispatch semaphore was more than one.
     * Or it became one and more before the specified timeout.
     * The counter is automatically decreased by one.
     *
     * Here, you can execute a task that needs a concurrency control.
     */

} else {

    /*
     * Because the counter of the dispatch semaphore was zero,
     * it has waited until the specified timeout.
     */

}
```

When a dispatch_semaphore_wait function returns zero, a task that needs a concurrency control can be executed safely. After you finish the task, you have to call the dispatch_semaphore_signal function to increase the counter of the dispatch semaphore by one. Listing 7–8 shows how to use a dispatch semaphore for the previous source code (Listing 7–6).

Listing 7–8. *Adding data to NSMutableArray using dispatch semaphore*

```
dispatch_queue_t queue =
    dispatch_get_global_queue(DISPATCH_QUEUE_PRIORITY_DEFAULT, 0);

/*
 * Create a dispatch semaphore
 *
 * Set the initial value 1 for the counter of the dispatch semaphore
 * to assure that only one thread will access the object of
 * NSMutableArray class at the same time.
 */

dispatch_semaphore_t semaphore = dispatch_semaphore_create(1);

NSMutableArray *array = [[NSMutableArray alloc] init];

for (int i = 0; i < 100000; ++i) {
    dispatch_async(queue, ^{

            /*
             * Wait for the dispatch semaphore
             *
             * Wait forever until the counter of the dispatch semaphore is one and
more.
             */

            dispatch_semaphore_wait(semaphore, DISPATCH_TIME_FOREVER);

            /*
             * Because the counter of the dispatch semaphore is one and more,
             * the counter is decreased by one and the program flow has returned from
             * the dispatch_semaphore_wait function.
             *
             * The counter of the dispatch semaphore is always zero here.
             *
             * Because only one thread can access the object of the NSMutableArray
class
             * at the same time, you can update the object safely.
             */

            [array addObject:[NSNumber numberWithInt:i]];

            /*
             * Because a task that needs concurrenct control is done,
             * you have to call the dispatch_semaphore_signal function
             * to increase the counter of the dispatch semaphore.
             *
             * If some threads are waiting for the counter of the dispatch_semaphore
             * incremented on dispatch_semaphore_wait, the first thread will be
started.
```

```
                 */

            dispatch_semaphore_signal(semaphore);
    });
}

 /*
  * Originally, because the dispatch semaphore isn't needed any more,
  * you have to release the dispatch semaphore.
  *
  * dispatch_release(semaphore);
  */
```

Next, let's see the dispatch_once function.

dispatch_once

The dispatch_once function is used to ensure that the specified task will be executed only once during the application's lifetime. Following is a typical source code to initialize something. It could be made elegant by using the dispatch_once function.

```
static int initialized = NO;

if (initialized == NO)
{

    /*
     * Initializing
     */

    initialized = YES;
}
```

With the dispatch_once function, it will be modified as follows.

```
static dispatch_once_t pred;

dispatch_once(&pred, ^{

    /*
     * Initializing
     */

});
```

There is not much difference between the two source codes. With the dispatch_once function, it works safely even in a multithreaded environment. The former source code is also safe in most cases. But on a multicore CPU, there is a slight chance that the 'initialized' variable might be read at the same time the value is overwritten. This will cause the initialization to be executed many times. However, no need to worry if you implemented it with the dispatch_once function. A dispatch_once function is useful to create a singleton object for a so-called "singleton pattern."

Dispatch I/O

To load a huge file, you might think it is faster if it is loaded as small blocks concurrently with using a global dispatch queue rather than in a normal way. With I/O hardware these days, it might be true. It might be faster if loaded concurrently than if loaded on one thread. To make it possible, you can use dispatch I/O and Dispatch Data. When you read or write a file with Dispatch I/O, one file is split into a certain size to be accessed on a global dispatch queue.

```
dispatch_async(queue, ^{/* loading the file from between 0 to 8191 byte. */});
dispatch_async(queue, ^{/*  loading the file from between 8192 to 16383 byte */});
dispatch_async(queue, ^{/* loading the file from between 16384 to 24575 byte */});
dispatch_async(queue, ^{/* loading the file from between 24576 to 32767 byte */});
dispatch_async(queue, ^{/* loading the file from between 32768 to 40959 byte */});
dispatch_async(queue, ^{/* loading the file from between 40960 to 49151 byte */});
dispatch_async(queue, ^{/* loading the file from between 49152 to 57343 byte */});
dispatch_async(queue, ^{/* loading the file from between 57344 to 65535 byte */});
```

Like the source code, loading will be done on each split block. Dispatch data can merge (or split) the loaded data more easily than doing it yourself. Let's see an example of a dispatch I/O and dispatch data by Apple as shown in Listing 7–9.

Listing 7–9. *Dispatch I/O*

```
pipe_q = dispatch_queue_create("PipeQ", NULL);
pipe_channel = dispatch_io_create(DISPATCH_IO_STREAM, fd, pipe_q, ^(int err){
      close(fd);
});

*out_fd = fdpair[1];

dispatch_io_set_low_water(pipe_channel, SIZE_MAX);

dispatch_io_read(pipe_channel, 0, SIZE_MAX, pipe_q,
      ^(bool done, dispatch_data_t pipedata, int err){
    if (err == 0)
    {
        size_t len = dispatch_data_get_size(pipedata);
        if (len > 0)
        {
            const char *bytes = NULL;
            char *encoded;

            dispatch_data_t md = dispatch_data_create_map(
                pipedata, (const void **)&bytes, &len);
            encoded = asl_core_encode_buffer(bytes, len);
            asl_set((aslmsg)merged_msg, ASL_KEY_AUX_DATA, encoded);
            free(encoded);
            _asl_send_message(NULL, merged_msg, -1, NULL);
            asl_msg_release(merged_msg);
            dispatch_release(md);
        }
    }

    if (done)
```

```
    {
        dispatch_semaphore_signal(sem);
        dispatch_release(pipe_channel);
        dispatch_release(pipe_q);
    }
});
```

This is taken from an Apple System Log API (Libc-763.11 gen/asl.c) source code. The dispatch_io_create function creates a dispatch I/O. It specifies a Block that is executed when an error occurs and a dispatch queue that executes the Block. A dispatch_io_set_low_water function sets the size of each reading (the data are split into this size). The dispatch_io_read function starts reading on the global dispatch queue. Whenever one of the split data blocks is read, the dispatch data are passed as the parameter of the Block that is set as the callback for reading finished in dispatch_io_read. So, the Block can scan or merge the dispatch data. If you want to read files bit faster than the normal way, try to use a dispatch I/O.

Summary

In this chapter, we learned how to use GCD API in detail. And we also learned:

- The relationship of the dispatch queue and thread

- How to execute a synchronized or asynchronized Block

- How to avoid a race condition

In the next chapter, we show the implementation of GCD giving us a deeper understanding of it.

Chapter 8

GCD Implementation

In this chapter, I explain how GCD is implemented in order to give you a better understanding of how it works. And then I explain one functionality of GCD called "data source," which relates to the XNU kernel event.

Dispatch Queue

This section shows how GCD is implemented. We especially look at the GCD structure and then see how a Block is executed on the dispatch queue.

Kernel-Level Implementation

From its functionality, we can guess that GCD uses the following components.

- A FIFO queue in the C language-level to manage the added Blocks
- Lightweight semaphore for concurrency control by atomic functions
- A container in the C language-level to manage threads

If that is all, it doesn't need kernel-level implementation.[1] In other words, if an application programmer could write application source code that has the same functionality using threads, GCD seems unnecessary. Why do we need GCD?

Again, let's see what Apple says.

> This technology takes the thread management code you would normally write in your own applications and moves that code down to the system level.

---

[1] Actually, there is an implementation of GCD ported for the common Linux operating system: Portable libdispatch `https://www.heily.com/trac/libdispatch`

It says that the thread management code is in the "system level," which means that it is done beyond the reach of the application programmer.

In fact, GCD has some system-level implementations called the XNU kernel that is a core of iOS and OS X. An application that manages threads by the application programmer can never have better performance than an application using GCD that is implemented in the XNU kernel-level. In other words, GCD is better than normal multithreaded programming with pthreads or NSThread. And, with GCD, you don't need to write the same code again and again (it's called a boilerplate code). You can concentrate on the task itself. Only good things happen! You should just use the GCD or NSOperationQueue class in the Cocoa Framework that uses GCD under the hood.

GCD Structure

Table 8–1 lists the software components that are used to implement dispatch queues.

Table 8–1. *Software components used for Dispatch Queue*

Component name	Feature
libdispatch	Dispatch Queue
Libc (pthreads)	pthread_Workqueue
XNU kernel	Workqueue

All the GCD APIs for application programmers are C language functions in the libdispatch library. A dispatch queue is a FIFO queue implemented as a struct and a linked list. This FIFO queue manages Blocks that are added by the dispatch_async function and the like. A Block isn't added to a FIFO queue directly. At first it is added to a struct of dispatch_continuation_t type, called dispatch continuation, and then it is added to a FIFO queue. A dispatch continuation is so-called execution context, which stores a dispatch group with which the Block is associated, and so on.

As you know, a dispatch queue can be a target by the dispatch_set_target_queue function. A dispatch queue is executed on its target dispatch queue. The targets can be linked in a row. The end of the link must be the main dispatch queue, one of the global dispatch queues, or a global dispatch queue that is prepared for each serial dispatch queue of various priorities. The main dispatch queue is a mechanism to execute Blocks in the RunLoop. There are not many exciting tricks there.

Global Dispatch Queue and pthread_workqueue

There are global dispatch queues as in the following list.

- Global Dispatch Queue (High priority)

- Global Dispatch Queue (Default priority)

- Global Dispatch Queue (Low priority)

- Global Dispatch Queue (Background priority)

- Global Dispatch Queue (High overcommit priority)

- Global Dispatch Queue (Default overcommit priority)

- Global Dispatch Queue (Low overcommit priority)

- Global Dispatch Queue (Background overcommit priority)

The four queues with overcommit priority are used as serial dispatch queues. As the name "overcommit" suggests, these dispatch queues create threads forcibly regardless of the system status. Each global dispatch queue uses its own pthread_workqueue. While GCD is initialized, the pthread_workqueue_create_np function initializes the pthread_workqueues.

A pthread_workqueue is a private pthread API in Libc. A pthread_workqueue initializes a workqueue in the XNU kernel by a bsdthread_register system call and a workq_open system call to get information about the workqueue. The XNU kernel has four workqueues.

- WORKQUEUE_HIGH_PRIOQUEUE

- WORKQUEUE_DEFAULT_PRIOQUEUE

- WORKQUEUE_LOW_PRIOQUEUE

- WORKQUEUE_BG_PRIOQUEUE

Each workqueue has a different priority (Figure 8–1). These priorities are equivalent to the four priorities of global dispatch queues.

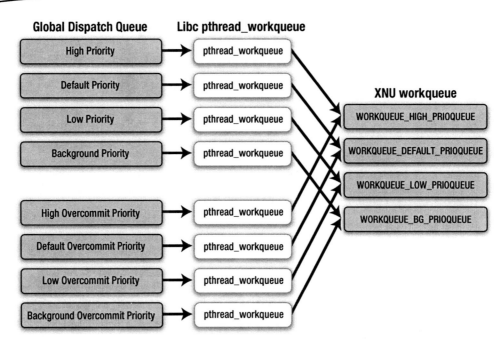

Figure 8–1. *Relationship of Global Dispatch Queue, pthread_workqueue, and workqueue*

Let's see how a Block is executed on a dispatch queue.

Executing Blocks

When a Block is executed on a global dispatch queue, libdispatch picks up a dispatch continuation from a FIFO queue, the global dispatch queue itself. It calls the pthread_workqueue_additem_np function with arguments of the global dispatch queue, workqueue information having the same priority as the global dispatch queue, and a callback function to execute the dispatch continuation. The pthread_workqueue_additem_np function notifies that an item to be executed is added to the workqueue, using the workq_kernreturn system call. When the XNU kernel gets the notification, it decides, based on the system status, whether it should create a thread. For a global dispatch queue with overcommit priority, a thread is created at any time. Here, the thread has almost the same meaning as a thread that is used in normal iOS or OS X programming, but some pthread APIs can't be used. For more information, see the "Compatibility with POSIX Threads" section in Apple's *Concurrency Programming Guide*.

The threads for workqueues are managed by a special thread scheduler that is implemented specially for workqueues. Its context switch is a bit different from the normal thread. This is one of the reasons we should use GCD. A thread for a workqueue calls a pthread_workqueue function. The function calls a callback function in libdispatch. Then it executes a Block in the dispatch continuation. When the Block is finished, a dispatch group is notified, and the dispatch continuation is released. Finally, it prepares to execute the next Block in the global dispatch queue. That is the rough execution flow of a dispatch queue.

Anyway, we've learned that it is impossible for an application programmer to have a more effective implementation than GCD.

Dispatch Source

In this section, we learn one more feature of GCD called the *dispatch source*. This is a useful functionality to handle kernel events from the application side. This is a low-level feature, although it might be useful in some applications. A dispatch source is a wrapper for a kqueue that is a very common feature in the BSD kernel. Kqueue is a mechanism to execute a task in the application program when an XNU kernel event occurs. It is very lightweight and does not consume many resources including CPU load. We can say that kqueue is the best mechanism to process an XNU kernel event on the application side. Dispatch source can handle the events listed in Table 8–2.

Table 8–2. *Types of Dispatch Sources*

Name	Description
DISPATCH_SOURCE_TYPE_DATA_ADD	Data are added
DISPATCH_SOURCE_TYPE_DATA_OR	"or" is used for the data
DISPATCH_SOURCE_TYPE_MACH_SEND	Sent via MACH port
DISPATCH_SOURCE_TYPE_MACH_RECV	Received via MACH port
DISPATCH_SOURCE_TYPE_PROC	Process-related event is detected
DISPATCH_SOURCE_TYPE_READ	A file descriptor became readable
DISPATCH_SOURCE_TYPE_SIGNAL	Got signal
DISPATCH_SOURCE_TYPE_TIMER	Timer
DISPATCH_SOURCE_TYPE_VNODE	File system modified
DISPATCH_SOURCE_TYPE_WRITE	A file descriptor became writable

When an event occurs, a task that is assigned to the event will be executed on the specified dispatch queue.

Listing 8–1 shows how an asynchronous file descriptor is read with DISPATCH_SOURCE_TYPE_READ.

Listing 8–1. *File reading using dispatch source*

```
__block size_t total = 0;
size_t size = how many bytes you want to get;
char *buff = (char *)malloc(size);
 /*
  * Set as an asynchronous (NONBLOCK) descripter for 'sockfd', a file descripter
  */
fcntl(sockfd, F_SETFL, O_NONBLOCK);

 /*
  * Obtain a global dispatch queue to add an event handler.
  */
dispatch_queue_t queue =
    dispatch_get_global_queue(DISPATCH_QUEUE_PRIORITY_DEFAULT, 0);

 /*
  * Create a dispatch source with READ event.
  */
dispatch_source_t source =
    dispatch_source_create(DISPATCH_SOURCE_TYPE_READ, sockfd, 0, queue);

 /*
  * Assign a task with the READ event.
  */
dispatch_source_set_event_handler(source, ^{
    /*
     * Get the available data size.
     */
    size_t available = dispatch_source_get_data(source);

    /*
     * Read data from the descriptor
     */
    int length = read(sockfd, buff, available);

    /*
     * When an error occurs, cancel the dispatch source.
     */
    if (length < 0) {
        /*
         * error handling
         */

        dispatch_source_cancel(source);
    }

    total += length;

    if (total == size) {

        /*
         * Process the buff
         */

        /*
         * Cancel the dispatch source to finalize it
         */
```

```
        dispatch_source_cancel(source);
    }
});

/*
 * Assign a task for the cancellation of the dispatch source
 */
dispatch_source_set_cancel_handler(source, ^{
    free(buff);
    close(sockfd);

    /*
     * Release the dispatch source itself
     */
    dispatch_release(timer);
});

/*
 * Resume the dispatch source
 */
dispatch_resume(source);
```

There is very similar source code for this example in a CFSocket, an asynchronous network API of the Core Foundation Framework. Because asynchronous network APIs in the Foundation Framework are implemented with the CFSocket, you can get the benefit of a dispatch source. In other words, you can get the benefit of GCD just by using the Foundation Framework.

Example Using Dispatch Source

To wrap up, let's see an example of a timer using DISPATCH_SOURCE_TYPE_TIMER (Listing 8–2). It can be used for a connection timeout in network programming.

Listing 8–2. *Timer using dispatch source*

```
/*
 * Create a dispatch source with DISPATCH_SOURCE_TYPE_TIMER
 *
 * When a specified time is elapsed, a task will be added to the main dispatch queue
 */
dispatch_source_t timer = dispatch_source_create(
    DISPATCH_SOURCE_TYPE_TIMER, 0, 0, dispatch_get_main_queue());

/*
 * Set the timer to 15 seconds later,
 * Without repeating,
 * Allow one-second delay
 */
dispatch_source_set_timer(timer,
    dispatch_time(DISPATCH_TIME_NOW, 15ull * NSEC_PER_SEC),
        DISPATCH_TIME_FOREVER, 1ull * NSEC_PER_SEC);

/*
 * Set a task to be executed when the specified time is passed.
 */
```

```
dispatch_source_set_event_handler(timer, ^{
    NSLog(@"wakeup!");

    /*
     * Cancel the dispatch source
     */
    dispatch_source_cancel(timer);
});

/*
 * Assign a task for the cancellation of the dispatch source
 */
dispatch_source_set_cancel_handler(timer, ^{
    NSLog(@"canceled");

    /*
     * Release the dispatch source itself
     */
    dispatch_release(timer);
});

/*
 * Resume the dispatch source
 */
dispatch_resume(timer);
```

When you saw the previous source code reading an asynchronous file descriptor or the source code of a timer, you might have noticed something.

A dispatch queue doesn't have the concept of "cancel." When a task is added to a dispatch queue, you can't remove it or cancel it. You might write a code to cancel it for yourself, give up the cancellation, or you might choose other APIs such as NSOperationQueue. With dispatch sources, you can cancel that. You can assign a task as a Block with a callback for cancellation. Because of that, it is easier to handle an event in the XNU kernel with a dispatch source than directly with kqueue. When you have to do something related to kqueue, you should use a dispatch source. It makes the source code simple.

Summary

In this chapter, we learned the implementation of the dispatch queue, and how to use dispatch source.

In this book, you've mastered ARC, Block, and GCD from the basics to the details with their implementations: ARC, the automatic memory management by the compiler, Block, as a new syntax to make application code unbelievably short, and GCD, the very effective multithread programming model.

When you understand these technologies and use them properly, your application will become highly responsive and of high quality. Please start using these technologies. I hope your great applications are on the App Store top 10 list!

Example of ARC, Blocks, and GCD

Let's see an example using ARC, Blocks, and GCD. The following source code reads data from a URL and displays the result on the main thread. That is a very typical use case in iOS applications so you can paste this as a part of your application. This shows you how ARC, Block, and GCD can be used for an application such as a twitter or Tumblr client.

The source code is explained with its comments.

```
NSString *url = @"http://images.apple.com/"
    "jp/iphone/features/includes/camera-gallery/03-20100607.jpg"

 /*
  * On the main thread, downloading data from the specified URL starts asynchronously.
  */

[ASyncURLConnection request:url completeBlock:^(NSData *data) {

    dispatch_queue_t queue =
        dispatch_get_global_queue(DISPATCH_QUEUE_PRIORITY_DEFAULT, 0);
    dispatch_async(queue, ^{

        /*
         * On a global dispatch queue, processing the downloaded data
         * It doesn't prevent the main thread, which means this task can take long.
         */

        dispatch_async(dispatch_get_main_queue(), ^{

            /*
             * Here, it uses the result on the main dispatch queue.
             * Displays the result on the user interface.
             */
        });
    });

} errorBlock:^(NSError *error) {
```

```
    /*
     * Error occurred
     */

    NSLog(@"error %@", error);
}];
```

Processing the downloaded data is executed on the other thread to avoid preventing the main thread. The dispatch_get_global_queue function obtains a global dispatch queue with default priority, and the dispatch_async function processes the data on the global dispatch queue. When the processing is finished, the user interface has to be updated on the main thread to show the result. This is done by the dispatch_get_main_queue function to obtain the main dispatch queue and by the dispatch_async function to execute the task.

By the way, should the downloading itself be implemented with GCD to run on the other threads to avoid preventing the main thread? The answer is no. For network programming, an asynchronous API is strongly recommended. Please see the following WWDC 2010 sessions.

■ WWDC 2010 Session 207—Network Apps for iPhone OS, Part 1

■ WWDC 2010 Session 208—Network Apps for iPhone OS, Part 2

These are the sessions about network programming. It definitely says "Threads Are Evil™" for network programming. When threads are used for network programming, it tends to use too many threads. For example, if a thread is created for each connection, stacks for each thread will consume too much memory instantly. There are asynchronous network APIs in the Cocoa Framework. Please make sure to use an asynchronous network API. You must not use threads for networks.

An ASyncURLConnection class in the source code is a class for network programming and has a base class NSURLConnection in the Foundation Framework, which is to load data asynchronously via a network. Let's see how the class is implemented.

ASyncURLConnection.h
```
#import <Foundation/Foundation.h>

 /*
  * By using typedef for a Block type variables,
  * Source code will have better readability.
  */

typedef void (^completeBlock_t)(NSData *data);
typedef void (^errorBlock_t)(NSError *error);

@interface ASyncURLConnection : NSURLConnection
{
     /*
      * Because ARC is enabled, all the variables below are
      * qualified with __strong  when it doesn't have an explicit qualifier.
      */
```

```objectivec
    NSMutableData *data_;
    completeBlock_t completeBlock_;
    errorBlock_t errorBlock_;
}

 /*
  * To give the source code better readability,
  * The typedefined Block type variable is used for the argument.
  */

+ (id)request:(NSString *)requestUrl
    completeBlock:(completeBlock_t)completeBlock
    errorBlock:(errorBlock_t)errorBlock;

- (id)initWithRequest:(NSString *)requestUrl
    completeBlock:(completeBlock_t)completeBlock
    errorBlock:(errorBlock_t)errorBlock;
@end
```

ASyncURLConnection.m

```objectivec
#import "ASyncURLConnection.h"

@implementation ASyncURLConnection

+ (id)request:(NSString *)requestUrl
    completeBlock:(completeBlock_t)completeBlock
    errorBlock:(errorBlock_t)errorBlock
{
    /*
     * If ARC is disabled,
     * This method should return an object after autorelease is called:
     *          * id obj = [[[self alloc] initWithRequest:requestUrl
     *    completeBlock:completeBlock errorBlock:errorBlock];
     * return [obj autorelease];
     *
     * Because this method name doesn't begin with alloc/new/copy/mutableCopy,
     * the returned object has been automatically registered in autoreleasepool.
     */

    return [[self alloc] initWithRequest:requestUrl
        completeBlock:completeBlock errorBlock:errorBlock];
}

- (id)initWithRequest:(NSString *)requestUrl
    completeBlock:(completeBlock_t)completeBlock
    errorBlock:(errorBlock_t)errorBlock
{
    NSURL *url = [NSURL URLWithString:requestUrl];
    NSURLRequest *request = [NSURLRequest requestWithURL:url];

    if ((self = [super initWithRequest:request
            delegate:self startImmediately:NO])) {
        data_ = [[NSMutableData alloc] init];

        /*
         * To make sure that you can use the passed Block safely,
         * the instance method 'copy' is called to put the Block on the heap.
```

```
                            */
                completeBlock_ = [completeBlock copy];
                errorBlock_ = [errorBlock copy];

                [self start];
        }

            /*
             * Member variables that have a __strong qualifier
             * have ownership of the created NSMutableData class object
             *
             * When the object is discarded, the strong references
             * of the member variables with the __strong qualifier disappear.
             * The NSMutableData class object and the Block will be released automatically.
             *
             * So, you don't need to implement the dealloc instance method explicitly.
             */

        return self;
}

- (void)connection:(NSURLConnection *)connection
    didReceiveResponse:(NSURLResponse *)response
{
    [data_ setLength:0];
}

- (void)connection:(NSURLConnection *)connection
    didReceiveData:(NSData *)data
{
    [data_ appendData:data];
}

- (void)connectionDidFinishLoading:(NSURLConnection *)connection
{
        /*
         * Execute the Block assigned as callback for downloading success.
         * The legacy delegate callback can be replaced by Block.
         */

        completeBlock_(data_);
}

- (void)connection:(NSURLConnection *)connection
    didFailWithError:(NSError *)error
{
        /*
         * Execute the Block that is assigned for error.
         */

        errorBlock_(error);
}

@end
```

When the downloading is finished or an error occurs, the NSURLConnection class calls a method on an object that is assigned to its delegate. The ASyncURLConnection class inherits the NSURLConnection class and Blocks can be set as callback for download finished and an error occurred. With this class, an application source code can be simpler. ARC manages the object of the NSMutableData class that is to store the downloaded data and the Blocks for callbacks properly. Because the member variables are qualified with __strong, you don't need to call the retain or release method explicitly, Actually, you can't call them in an ARC-enabled environment. And, you don't need to implement the dealloc instance method.

You must realize that ARC, Blocks, and Grand Central Dispatch are powerful even in such a simple source code.

References

This appendix provides a list of references that you should find helpful. They are listed in three categories for ARC, Blocks, and Grand Central Dispatch.

References for ARC

Transitioning to ARC Release Notes

▨ http://developer.apple.com/library/mac/#releasenotes/ObjectiveC
/RN-TransitioningToARC/_index.html

ARC Programming Guide by Apple

When you want to know something about ARC, you should read this document first. If you're reading this book before it, it is ok :-), but you should read it later.

LLVM Document—Automatic Reference Counting

▨ http://clang.llvm.org/docs/AutomaticReferenceCounting.html

This document is something like the specification of ARC. When you want to make sure of its specification, please check this out.

Advanced Memory Management Programming Guide

▨ http://developer.apple.com/library/ios/documentation/Cocoa/
Conceptual/MemoryMgmt/Articles/MemoryMgmt.html

This is a document by Apple that explains memory management with reference counting in detail.

Getting Started: Building and Running Clang

- http://clang.llvm.org/get_started.html

- Subversion repository http://llvm.org/svn/llvm-project/cfe/trunk

This explains how to get the source code of clang (LLVM compiler 3.0), which is the compiler supporting ARC. The repository of the source code is there, too. For example, the following source codes in the repository have the implementation to achieve ARC.

- llvm/tools/clang/lib/CodeGen/CGObjC.cpp

- llvm/tools/clang/lib/CodeGen/CGObjCMac.cpp

objc4 version 493.9

- http://www.opensource.apple.com/source/objc4/objc4-493.9/

This is an implementation of the Objective-C runtime library by Apple. The source code is available. The Objective-C runtime APIs that are explained in the above document "LLVM Document—Automatic Reference Counting" are implemented in this library.

ARC-related APIs are mostly in the following file.

- runtime/objc-arr.mm

APIs that are related to the __weak qualifier are in:

- runtime/objc-weak.mm

GNUstep libobjc2 version 1.5

- http://gnustep.blogspot.com/2011/07/gnustep-objective-c-runtime-15-released.html

- http://thread.gmane.org/gmane.comp.lib.gnustep.general/36358

- http://svn.gna.org/viewcvs/gnustep/libs/libobjc2/1.5/

libobjc2 is an implementation of the Objective-C runtime library supporting ARC by the GNUstep project. It is equivalent to objc4, that is, the Objective-C runtime library by Apple.

References for Blocks

APPLE'S EXTENSIONS TO C

- http://www.open-std.org/jtc1/sc22/wg14/www/docs/n1370.pdf

This is an overview document about C language extensions that are implemented by Apple. We can see that the basic ideas of ARC, __strong qualifier and __weak qualifier, have already been implemented during the Blocks implementation.

BLOCKS PROPOSAL, N1451

■   http://www.open-std.org/jtc1/sc22/wg14/www/docs/n1451.pdf

Here is a proposal of Blocks for C99, the C language specification "ISO/IEC 9899:1999(E) Programming Language-C (Second Edition)." It is proposed by Apple to the ISO/IEC JTC1/SC22/WG14 international standardization working group for the C programming language, an organization to standardize the C language. At this moment, there does not seem to be activity to add Blocks to the C standard.

Presentation About Blocks

■   http://www.open-std.org/jtc1/sc22/wg14/www/docs/n1457.pdf

This is a presentation about Blocks by Apple. It seems to be used to promote Blocks to the WG14 working group. It is useful as an overview of Blocks.

Language Specification for Blocks

■   http://clang.llvm.org/docs/BlockLanguageSpec.txt

This is a Blocks language specification included in LLVM. By reading this along with "Block Implementation Specification" below, you can learn how to implement a compiler and a runtime library supporting Blocks. If you want to make a compiler support Blocks, you must read this.

Block Implementation Specification

■   http://clang.llvm.org/docs/Block-ABI-Apple.txt

■   Here is a Blocks implementation specification that is included in LLVM. When you have a compiler supporting Blocks, but don't have a runtime library, you can find a solution by reading this.

libclosure version 53

■   http://www.opensource.apple.com/source/libclosure/libclosure-53/

libclosure is a runtime library for Blocks by Apple. This library provides APIs for Blocks such as Block_copy and Block_release functions.

plblocks

▨   http://code.google.com/p/plblocks/

It is a runtime library to support Blocks on old OSs, which don't support Blocks, such as OS X 10.5 Snow Leopard and iOS 3.0. On the old OSs, the runtime libraries don't have Block-related functions such as Block_copy or Block_release. By using its own implementation in plblocks, Blocks will work on the old OSs.

References for Grand Central Dispatch

libdispatch version 187.5

▨   http://www.opensource.apple.com/source/libdispatch/libdispatch-187.5/

libdispatch is a library by Apple to provide GCD API, such as dispatch queues, and the like.

Libc version 763.11

▨   http://www.opensource.apple.com/source/Libc/Libc-763.11/

The pthread_workqueue API is implemented. This API stems from the GCD pthread_workqueue.

API-related source codes are:

▨   pthreads/pthread.c

▨   pthreads/pthread_workqueue.h

xnu version 1699.22.81

▨   http://www.opensource.apple.com/source/xnu/xnu-1699.22.81/

This is the source code of the XNU kernel, which is a core of Mac OS X and iOS. You can see the workqueue implementations of the XNU kernel in the following source code.

▨   bsd/kern/pthread_synch.c

▨   osfmk/kern/thread.c

libdispatch project page

▨   http://libdispatch.macosforge.org/

This is a libdispatch open source project page by Apple. You can read libdispatch mailing lists, porting information of libdispatch to the other OSs, and so on.

libdispatch Porting Project

- https://www.heily.com/trac/libdispatch

This is the project page for porting projects of libdispatch. It distributes the libdispatch with modifications to compile on other OSs such as the following.

- FreeBSD

- Linux

- Solaris

- Windows

If you have to write an application for an operating system other than Mac OS X or iOS, I recommend using it.

Index